TERMS OF THE POLITICAL

FORDHAM UNIVERSITY PRESS NEW YORK 2013

COMMONALITIES

Timothy Campbell, series editor

TERMS OF THE POLITICAL

Community, Immunity, Biopolitics

ROBERTO ESPOSITO

Translated by Rhiannon Noel Welch

The translation of this work has been funded by SEPS Segretariato Europeo per le Pubblicazioni Scientifiche

Via Val d'Aposa 7 - 40123 Bologna - Italy
seps@seps.it - www.seps.it

Library of Congress Cataloging-in-Publication Data is available from the publisher.

Printed in the United States of America

15 14 13   5 4 3 2 1

First edition

CONTENTS

TERMS OF THE POLITICAL

INTRODUCTION: BIOPOLITICS AND COMMUNITY IN ROBERTO ESPOSITO

VANESSA LEMM

Foucault once said that political theory had still not reckoned with the end of sovereign power. In like fashion, one can say that political theory is only just now starting to confront itself and its languages with the consequences caused by the entrance of biology and biological considerations into questions of government. Roberto Esposito is perhaps the contemporary thinker who has gone furthest in questioning the traditional categories of political thought in light of the emergence of biopolitics. In this accessible collection of essays, he presents his own philosophical enterprise in terms of bridging deconstruction with biopolitics. Esposito is perhaps best known for his project of deconstructing the categories of modern political thought—all of which turn around the idea of immunity—by appealing to the subversive potential of the idea of community. In his recently translated volume *Bios: Biopolitics and Philosophy*, he embarks on the project of providing an affirmative biopolitics. But what is the connection between the question of biopolitics and the fact of community? How can biopolitics help us identify the limits and possibilities of community? What is the urgency of this question today? In this introduction I shall try to indicate how these essays move from a deconstruction of modernity's individualism toward a new affirmative biopolitics of community. Several commentators have recently argued that Esposito's understanding of biopolitics turns on the relation between philosophy and life, that his treatment of biopolitics and community begins and ends in philosophy. But how does Esposito understand the relation between theory and practice? Part of the answer to this question is found in the way in which Esposito understands the relation of the art of writing to the tasks of philosophical reflection today. I believe that an analysis of the latter will also provide elements to understand the new relation he posits between community and biopolitics that makes up his idea of an affirmative biopolitics.

By an *affirmative biopolitics*, I here mean two things: a new way of understanding the experience of freedom and the ways in which the experience of freedom circumscribes Esposito's own position as a writer. *Terms of the Political* is a book whose chapters can be read in any order and where chapters stand on their own but at the same time can together make up a whole. The book is divided into eleven chapters and all of them share at least three distinguishing features: First, every chapter is dedicated to a particular question, where the treatment of the question does not reach a final answer but rather complicates the question by drawing our attention to what has been forgotten, repressed, or destroyed. This is why, and here is the second distinguishing feature, all of the chapters end on openness and the impossibility of closure: They lead us to the unknown, the yet to come, the blurriness of the horizon of the future. *Terms of the Political* thus does not pretend to answer the questions of our time, to solve them once and for all, but rather offers new perspectives on our contemporary situation that make us think differently about the world we live in. In so doing, the emergence of new and common forms of life and thought becomes possible.

The reader will find only one chapter that inevitably, or rather necessarily, ends on an affirmative tone, and this is the chapter dedicated to the question of freedom or, better, to the experience of freedom. I will return to this chapter in more detail below. For now, let me just say that the affirmation of freedom is necessary for Esposito insofar as it circumscribes his own position as a writer. Here the experience of writing confronts the writer with the impossibility of coming to terms with the challenges entailed in each question. At the same time, writing imposes itself as a necessity from which the author cannot escape. Paradoxically, it is the affirmation of both the impossibility and necessity of writing that gives rise to the experience of freedom. Yet impossibility and necessity are also precisely those features that Esposito ascribes to the concept of community. Community, like writing, is both necessary and impossible: Community is a necessity to the degree that it constitutes our originary condition, the fact that we have always existed in common. Community is impossible, however, insofar as it can never be fully realized. Community is a debt, a flaw, a lack. From this perspective, what we have in common by necessity is the impossibility of realizing community.

Lastly, all of the book's chapters exemplify Esposito's conception of community in that each puts into communication or in common concepts that have otherwise been thought to be irreconcilable, excluding or opposing each other. This is the case whether we are speaking of community and law (chapter 1), community and violence (chapter 11), immunity and freedom (chapter 4), immunity and violence (chapter 5), politics and human nature (chapter 8), philosophy and biopolitics (chapter 6), and so on. All of these pairings reflect a combination of the concepts of immunity and community, revealing that the distinctive feature and overall objective of Esposito's philosophical project remains that of rethinking the relation between these terms. In this sense, Esposito's work can without doubt be ascribed to what is currently being referred to as the new thinking of community.

Only one chapter does not call for a communication between concepts, signified by the *and* found in the titles of all the other chapters, and that is chapter 9, "Totalitarianism or Biopolitics." I take the *or* in the title of this chapter to mean the necessity of making an inevitable decision: either totalitarianism or biopolitics. The exclusive *or* calls for a decision, a decision that designates the new starting point of Esposito's investigation as beyond the deconstruction of modern political categories but that is also a decision that he urges his readers to make. The chapter thus stands apart and offers the hermeneutical key to an understanding of what is at stake in Esposito's rethinking of community. In the first three essays, Esposito argues that human beings have always rightly associated community with the threat of violence. The violence inherent in community is related to the incapacity of community merely to preserve the life of its members. Esposito attributes this feature of community to the root of the term, *munus*, which contains a plurality of meanings: debt, duty, or obligation and gift. Accordingly, Esposito deduces that community—or *cum-munus*—stands for a reciprocal obligation imposed on the individual members of the community to stand to each other in a relation of gift giving, which may take the form of a particular office or simply the donation of goods. From this perspective, the law of community is a law that prescribes nothing else but the exigency of community itself, the expenditure of self for the other. Additionally, Esposito hypothesizes that the law of community constitutes an originary condition of human existence, given that we have always existed in common; that is, we come into the world always already under this law and under this debt, or guilt.

This leads him to another characteristic of community, which is tied to its inhospitality with the claims of individual self-preservation. If being in common is our first necessity, it is also equally true, according to Esposito, that this necessity has never been realized and is in fact unrealizable. As such, community reflects an infinite lack, an unpayable debt: What we have always already in common is this very lack of community. What we have in common is the impossibility of realizing community, or, in the words of Esposito, the finitude of our existence, our being mortal and in time. Esposito traces this double feature of community as both impossibility and a necessity from Rousseau to Kant and Heidegger, urging us to rethink the fact that otherness constitutes us from deep within. The insight into the antinomy of community leads Esposito to reflect on the relationship between melancholy and community. He argues that melancholy is something that contains and determines community itself, according to which community designates the originary gap that separates the existence of the community from its own essence. Esposito argues that community is a non-entity, a non-being that precedes and cuts every subject wresting an identification from the self and submitting him or her to an irreducible alterity. The communal dimension of life sweeps away individual life—that is, by the lack of identity, individuality and difference. Melancholy reveals community to be always different from what it wants to be. Community carries within itself its own nonbelonging to itself, its impropriety. Such a thought of community confronts us with the still open question of how to translate this impropriety of community into the reality of our subjectivity. Against this threat of undifferentiated community, Esposito claims in chapters 3, 4, and 5 that modern political philosophy erects an enormous apparatus of immunization. By *immunization*, Esposito understands a progressive interiorization of exteriority. If community is our "outside," immunization is what brings us back within ourselves by cutting off all contact with the outside. Immunization is therefore understood as a frontier, a dividing line, a term or limit (of the political) that protects individual life from the demands of community.

The deconstruction of modern political categories turns on Esposito's discovery of the category of immunization as the key term of our political condition, as the term that most profoundly characterizes our time. *Immunization* refers to the particular situation that saves someone from the risk to which the entire community is exposed. In these essays, Esposito centers his attention on two particular immunitary devices: the ideas of subjective rights or personal liberties in chapters 3 through 5, and the idea of personhood in chapter 8. Whether we declare that freedom has already been realized in liberal democracies or belongs to a far-off future, we remain within a subjectivist metaphysical framework wherein the political scene is occupied by a preformed and predefined subject—the individual—who regards freedom as an object to define or conquer, to possess or extend. According to these accounts, freedom is a quality, a faculty, or a good to be acquired, appropriated, and constituted as subjective property such that the subject becomes the proprietor of himself or herself: "proper" and no longer "common." The outcome of this subjectivist foundation in both philosophical and historical terms reduces the horizon of the sense of the political, impoverishing it, whether politics is reduced to order, as in Hobbes, to sovereignty, as in Rousseau, or to the state, as in Hegel. All of these quintessentially modern political philosophies perform a logical passage from freedom to necessity, thereby showing how, in the name of protecting individual life and liberty, it is these very features that end up being imperiled.

A similar phenomenon arises with the idea of person in chapter 11. Esposito asks how it is possible that, at a time when the normative reference to the value of the person is upheld in all languages, the right to life is threatened more than ever before. According to Esposito, it is not a question of the restricted, partial, or incompatible extension of the ideology of the person; instead, the invasiveness of that ideology, its excess, produces such counterfactual outcomes. Esposito traces the category of the person back to its Christian and Roman origins, where he discovers that this category cannot fill the gap between "rights" and "humanity." Rather, the very category of personhood makes something like human rights impossible because such a category produces and widens the gap between its constitutive terms. In fact, his etymological and genealogical analysis reveals that the category of the person is based on a double separation: It first divides human life into a personal life and an animal life and, second, the category draws a dividing line with the human individual, separating out an irrational part that needs to be dominated and ruled over by a rational part. Those who are incapable of such self-rule are not worthy of accessing to the category of personhood. Accordingly, Esposito concludes that every attribution of personality always implicitly contains a reification of the impersonal biological layer from which it distances itself. Only when human beings can be assimilated to things does it become necessary to define others as persons.

The examples of subjective freedom and of personhood show that through immunization the violence of community does not disappear but is rather incorporated into the same apparatus that ought to do away with it. The idea of immunity, necessary for the protection of individual life, if carried past a certain threshold or limit, ends up attacking itself: Where immunitary devices characterize politics, modern politics becomes characterized by autoimmunitary effects in which the immune system becomes so strong that it turns against the very mechanism that it should defend and winds up destroying it. Esposito's analysis of late modernity is centered on the deconstruction of immunity in the form of autoimmune reactions. Now, the idea of autoimmunity—which features prominently in Derridean deconstruction—has the remarkable property of describing a process of destruction of individuality which at the same time harbors the preservation of this individuality. This is similar to what the idea of immunity revealed— namely, that what is intended to protect individuality may end up destroying it. Thus, autoimmunity, the radicalization of immunity to the point that an immunity is set up against what immunizes, should not be merely understood negatively, as the harbinger of autoimmune diseases that literally kill individuality. Rather, immunity should be seen, according to Esposito, also as a way for the individual to open up to what is threatening to him or her in order to alleviate the grip that one's own self-protection has over the individual: as a way of protecting oneself from too much protection. It is in this other sense that autoimmunity prepares the transition from deconstruction to affirmative biopolitics.

The radicalization of immunity in late modernity corresponds for Esposito to that process that Foucault identified as the ever more intense and direct involvement that is established between political dynamics and human life. Once the life of the human species becomes the object of political preservation and thus of immunization, one conclusion—which is typically thanatopolitical—becomes inevitable: that life can be preserved only at the cost of killing other life. Furthermore, in order for this killing to be achieved "normally"—that is, medically—it becomes necessary to bring down all of the earlier defense mechanisms that centered on subjective rights: We find ourselves in the midst of Nazism as biopolitics. Here the importance of the analysis of Nazism is preface to affirmative biopolitics, which Esposito takes up in chapter 7.

Esposito suggests that the discourse of biopolitics may not necessarily end in the destruction of life. He applies to life the logic of autoimmunity: If the task of immunizing life itself is what drives modern politics into its totalitarian tailspin, then it is just possible that, having let life into politics, we must learn to let life show us how to protect ourselves from too much protection and immunization. Here Esposito parts ways with Heidegger and in chapter 8 welcomes an aspect of contemporary antihumanism that Heidegger saw with preoccupation—namely, the question of the animality of the human being.

Against the self-destructive tendency of immunity, Esposito suggests that immunity must make itself again the custodian and producer of life. Immunity must be made not a barrier of separation but a filter of relations with what implores it from the outside. Esposito argues that for this reversal to occur we need to return to the term that holds together the two horizons of meaning for com-munity and im-munity. Esposito traces in the term *munus* the meanings of donation, expropriation, and alteration. In order to provoke the reversal that makes immunity not a function of separation but a function of relation, community and immunity ought to be placed in a reciprocal relation: to have community refer to difference and to have immunity refer to contamination. This reciprocal relation between community and immunity is what Esposito claims happens in our bodies and in all organ transplants and it is what happens in the experience of freedom.

In order to understand this alternative strategy that leads toward an affirmative biopolitics, Esposito argues that it is absolutely crucial to understand the role played by totalitarianism, and in particular by Nazism, for philosophical thinking about life and politics. Esposito devotes at least three chapters of this book (chapters 7, 8, and 9) to this question. Nazism, on Esposito's interpretation, represents the most virulent autoimmunitary disease of modernity: the moment in which biological life enters directly into politics as its privileged object, causing the transition from the immunitary preservation of individual life to the autoimmunitary killing of life and destruction of immunitary devices in the name of preserving the life of a "race" and a "people."

So far I have been speaking of the way in which a biopolitics of community requires a philosophical strategy that places in communication and in common a series of concepts that are usually believed to be opposed to each other. For Esposito, as I noted above, one opposition cannot be placed in common—namely, the opposition between totalitarianism and biopolitics. Philosophy today must begin by making an inevitable decision: either totalitarianism or biopolitics. The philosophical gesture of opposing, without mediation, biopolitics to totalitarianism is a provocative one because we are accustomed, from Hannah Arendt or Emmanuel Lévinas onward, to think about totalitarianism as the collapsing of spiritual or existential categories into biological ones. Doing so, one would be tempted to identify rather than oppose totalitarianism to biopolitics. Yet for Esposito, who is on this point very close to intuitions worked out by Antonio Negri, life is a matter of placing things in common, of opening communication between opposites. Against this backdrop, totalitarianism appears as a function of cutting off some parts of the whole from all community and all communication, and in that sense totalitarianism is a profoundly "spiritualist" social formation, entirely opposed to the community of life, and thus also to biopolitics.

The inclusive *and* of community and immunity, and the exclusive *either/or* of totalitarianism and biopolitics reflect two philosophical strategies found in *Terms of the Political*. Esposito hopes to reverse the relation that modern political philosophy established between community and immunity. Whereas the exclusive *either/or* stands at the center of a new and affirmative strategy for immunity, the inclusive *and/and* reflects a new and affirmative strategy of community. The experience of freedom in turn features an example of a successful reversal of the relation between community and immunity from an excluding and opposing relationship toward an inclusive and affirmative relationship.

In chapters 3 and 5, Esposito argues that the problem of our times is that there exists a barrier between language and politics: politics escapes language; language no longer has words for politics. This political aphasia not only is representative of our historical situation but in fact concerns all of modern political philosophy and its constitutively metaphysical character.

Esposito goes on to observe that the metaphysical element of modern political philosophy lies primarily in leveling the complexity of the sense horizons of concepts of political philosophy. Discarding such a frontal approach to the categories of politics, Esposito urges us to interrogate the categories of politics obliquely, thus entering the recessed layers of their meanings, bringing out what remains unthought in them. In contrast to the manifest meaning of political categories, which is always univocal, monolinear, and self-enclosed, Esposito argues that their underlying sense is much more complex, often contradictory, and capable of containing reciprocal opposing elements, antinomian characteristics—a genuine conflict for the conquest of a more weighty significance. Esposito thus approaches categories from the Heraclitean idea of the coincidence of opposites. This is the idea that we may be joined together, and we may live in common, not thanks to homogeneity but because of our distinction and diversity.

A return to the Heraclitean way of thinking requires divesting ourselves of the old philosophies of history and all of the conceptual paradigms to which they refer. We need to, as it were, immunize ourselves against the metaphysical presuppositions underlying modern political philosophy without, for all that, reverting to "another beginning" in Pre-Socratic thinking, which is the answer that Heidegger gives to the critique of modernity. Similarly, Antonio Negri advances the idea of an alter modernity—turning around the figures of Machiavelli, Spinoza, and Marx—which allows him to critique modern philosophy of history without having to return to the ancients. Esposito notes in chapter 6 that we can find immunity to modern philosophy of history by adopting Foucault's idea of an "ontology of the present." This idea protects us against ideological readings of the present that refute or negate the present, seeking to abandon it in favor of an unrealizable utopia. On the contrary, and in continuity with Esposito's genealogical approach to the concepts of politics, the idea of an "ontology of the present" requires inverting the notion of the possible that the present contains, making the present the basis for a different reading of reality.

According to Esposito, Foucault's ontology of the present leads us toward an inevitable choice between totalitarianism and biopolitics understood as two different perspectives on the present. Whereas totalitarianism stands for the perspective of the history of philosophy that subordinates historical dynamics to the logic of a given philosophy, biopolitics perceives history as philosophy that grasps an element or a character that is itself philosophical within certain historical events. Under the paradigm of biopolitics, meaning is no longer impressed upon historical events from the outside but is something that originates from and is made up of these events themselves. Unlike Arendt, who sees the entry of life into politics as a preamble for the depoliticization of human existence, Esposito views the same entry of life as a way to pluralize the meaning of politics. The strength of the biopolitical perspective, according to Esposito, resides precisely in its capacity to exploit the reserves of sense withheld by the mixing of the languages of politics and biology, which originally tended to be kept apart in the tradition of political philosophy. Accordingly, Esposito sees in the paradigm of biopolitics a reflection of the Heraclitean idea that we are joined together by opposition and difference rather than by homogeneity and equality. Or, in the words of Nietzsche, that the world is will to power where *will to power* acts as a relational term which cannot be reduced to a unitary self-identical structure. Rather, the world calls for a plurality of meanings invested by a multiplicity of different perspectives in continuous conflict with each other.

The decision between totalitarianism and biopolitics, moreover, leads Esposito to reject the equivalency between communism and fascism within the more general category of totalitarianism. From the perspective of biopolitics, the twentieth century, and indeed the course of modernity, cannot be determined or decided by the antithesis between totalitarianism and democracy, where totalitarianism and communism are thought together in opposition to the pairing between liberalism and democracy. For Esposito, it is precisely Foucault's discovery that liberalism is the form taken by biopolitical domination in late modernity that shows that the terms *liberal* and *democracy* are contradictory: for the government of life required by liberalism is contrary to the principle of equality that makes democracy possible. Indeed, for Esposito the modern understanding of democracy as spelled out in chapter 10, with its foundational distinctions between private and public, nature and artifice, is questioned at the root once it is bodies that replace the abstract subjectivity of the juridical persona. What needs to be thought instead is a new conjunction of democracy and communism, on the one hand, and of totalitarianism and liberalism, on the other. However, in order to save communism from falling back into philosophy of history, one needs to think of the alliance between communism and democracy from the perspective of an affirmative biopolitics of community.

The second philosophical strategy, which I have called the strategy of inclusion, entails that we move concepts out from the closed off and exclusive logic of immunity to the open and inclusive one of community such that *immunity* refers to contagion and *community* to difference. This shift requires from us to conceive community no longer as something to which we return or something to which we aspire. Community is neither origin nor a telos, neither goal nor an end, and neither presupposition nor destination. Instead, community is the condition, both singular and plural, of our complete existence. In order to better understand what kind of shift Esposito has in mind, it is useful to discuss two examples found in *Terms of the Political*: first, the shift from thanatopolitics to affirmative biopolitics and, second, the shift from freedom understood as an immunitary device to a relational-contagious experience.

In order to reintroduce the power of life into politics, instead of subjecting life to the direction of politics and thereby reversing a politics of death into a politics of life, we must, according to Esposito, rethink biopolitics from within the thanatopolitical paradigm. Esposito distinguishes three features of Nazi thanatopolitics: first, the absolute normalization of life—that is, the imprisonment of bios within the law of its own destruction; second, the double enclosure of the body, or the homicidal and suicidal immunization of the German people within the figure of the single racially purified body; and, third, the suppression of birth, which he sets out in chapter 7. Against these mechanisms, Esposito upholds, first, a conception of the norm that is immanent to bodies; second, a break with the closed and organic idea of a political body in favor of the multiplicity of the flesh of the world; and, third, a politics of birth intended as a continual production of difference with respect to only practice of identity. In all three cases, Esposito employs the same strategy: He begins with an immunitary device that has turned out to be deadly and reverses it into a device that can take on again the function of being the custodian and protector of life. This reversal is each time achieved by restoring the common root—the *munus*—of a given immunitary *dispositif*. As such, immunity stands no longer in opposition but in a reciprocal relationship to community.

The second example concerns the experience of freedom and personhood I discussed earlier, found in chapter 5. As we saw above, freedom and personhood are both subject to the same closure as community—that is, a preventive interiorization of the outside, a neutralizing appropriation. The immunity constituted by subjective freedom ends up giving way to the power of supraindividual constructions such as the modern state, which trample these same freedoms; likewise, the immunity constituted by the juridical category of person winds up giving way to global normative orders that cast into crisis the very idea of human rights. Esposito's deconstruction of the concepts of subjective freedom and personhood aims at reversing the movement from necessity back to freedom. Esposito clearly hopes to set in motion such a reversal through a return to the double meaning of freedom as love and friendship, according to which freedom exists in and as a relationship and not as an individual possession to be conquered and defended. Here, again, the deconstructive moment is joined to the biopolitical moment, since according to Esposito this powerfully affirmative sense of freedom is altogether biological and physical. The original root of *freedom*—from the Indo-European *leuth*—contains no reference to an absence of interference (as in the modern idea of subjective freedom) but instead refers to a movement of expansion, blossoming, or common growth that brings separate individuals together. In other words, it restores the meaning of freedom to the horizon of a common life. However, restoring the common dimension of freedom does not mean giving up its individual dimension. On the contrary, for Esposito, freedom designates the singular dimension of community: the part of community that resists immunization, that is not identical to itself, and that remains open to difference. Thus in the experience of freedom, community refers to difference and immunity to relation/contagion.

In chapter 10, "Toward a Philosophy of the Impersonal," Esposito argues that the deconstruction of the category of person requires an appeal to the impersonality of justice, writing, and animal life. Esposito links each gesture to three names of philosophy from the twentieth century: Simone Weil, Maurice Blanchot, and Gilles Deleuze. Whereas Weil thinks universal justice from the perspective of the impersonal, Blanchot conceives of writing as the creation of an opening of the impersonal, and Deleuze deconstructs the idea of the person by claiming animality as our most intrinsic nature, worth bringing back to light the animal in man, in every man and all men, which signifies multiplicity, plurality, and metamorphosis. In this chapter, the practice of deconstruction seems to pass over entirely into a politics of life. The question remains, which of these strategies or gestures is most radical? Whereas the appeal to an indeconstructible instance of justice or writing—as Derrida has shown throughout his work—is essential to the practice of deconstruction, the appeal to the impersonality of animal life may simply be a step beyond deconstruction itself. The work of Esposito moves back and forth between these gestures without ever deciding itself on any one of them. In this sense, Esposito leaves us with the open question of whether an affirmative biopolitics is simply the last figure of the deconstruction of metaphysical categories or whether the "becoming animal" of and within man may herald a future in which our community with radical otherness will no longer stand in need of metaphysics and thus, also, in need of its deconstruction.

THE LAW OF COMMUNITY

I'd like to reflect on community beginning with the word's original Latin root. The meaning that all etymological dictionaries suggest as most probable is the one that combines *cum* with *munus* (or *munia*). Such a derivation is important insofar as it designates precisely what holds the members of a community together. These members are not bound by just any relationship, but precisely by a *munus*—a "task," "duty," or "law." According to the other meaning of the term (which is closer to the first than it might seem), they are bound by a "gift," but a gift that is to be given rather than received. Therefore, even in this second case, they are bound by an "obligation." Members of a community are such if and because they are bound by a common law.

But what kind of law is it? What is the law to which community binds us? Or, more precisely, what "puts us in common"? We don't have to imagine anything outside of community itself, as if community exists before law, or law precedes community. Community is one with law in the sense that common law prescribes nothing else but the exigency of community itself. To use a still-inadequate expression, this is the primary content of the law of community: We need community. Here again, one must not think of a voice, like an external injunction, that addresses us from elsewhere but of something more inherent. We need community because it is the very locus or, better, the transcendental condition of our existence, given that we have always existed in common. The law of community is thus understood as the exigency according to which we feel obligated not to lose this originary condition—or, worse, not to turn it into its opposite. This is because not only is this risk ever present but it constitutes us as much as the law that puts us on guard against it. If we have always existed in the law, it is because we have always existed in "guilt," one might say, echoing Paul of Tarsus.[1] We have always existed in the forgetfulness and the perversion of the common law. From this point of view, which one mustn't take up separately from but together with the first, we ought to say not only that community has never been realized but that it is unrealizable. This, in spite of the necessity that requires community; in spite of the fact that in a certain sense community is constantly present. Yet it is unrealizable precisely because of this fact. How are we to realize something that precedes every possible realization? How are we to constitute something that already constitutes us? Within this paradox we can attempt an initial definition of community as that which is both necessary and impossible for us. Impossible and necessary. Something that determines us at a distance and in difference from our very selves, in the rupture of our subjectivity, in an infinite lack, in an unpayable debt, an irremediable fault [difetto]. We might even use the more loaded expression of "crime" [delitto], if we refer to the meaning of delinquere as "lacking something": We are lacking that which constitutes us as a community, so much so that we must conclude that what we have in common is precisely this lack of community.[2] As I've stated elsewhere, we are a community made up of those who do not have community.[3] The law of community is inseparable from the community of law, debt, or guilt, as illustrated by all the narratives that locate the origin of society in precisely such a common crime, wherein the victim (that is, the one that we lose, or the one that we never had) is no "primordial father" but the community itself, which nevertheless constitutes us transcendentally.

Such a more or less explicit awareness did not emerge recently but instead recurs throughout the great philosophical tradition beginning, at least, with Rousseau. His entire oeuvre proclaims, or, rather, cries out, this terrible truth: Community is both necessary and impossible. Human history harbors this wound, which corrodes and voids it from within. Our history is only interpretable in proportion to this "impossibility" from which it nevertheless originates, in the form of a necessary betrayal: We inhabit the margin between what we owe and what we can do. So much so that when we do attempt to construct, realize, or effect community, we inevitably end up turning it into its exact opposite—a community of death and the death of community. Let's begin with the first point—we need community. Community is our res, meaning precisely that we are the sole bearers of responsibility for it. One might condense Rousseau's incessant critique of the Hobbesian paradigm into just such a proposition. Rousseau observes that "when isolated men, however numerous they may be, are subjected one after another to a single person . . . they form, if you will, an aggregation, but not an association, for they have neither public property nor a body politic," he is actually accusing Hobbes of not only overlooking but indeed violently excluding every idea of community.[4] This is true insofar as the English philosopher unites naturally conflicting individuals within the great body of the Leviathan. If the glue that holds such individuals together is nothing but communal fear, the result can be nothing but communal servitude, or the exact opposite of community. Community is precisely what is sacrificed on the altar of individual self-preservation: Hobbes's individuals can save their own lives only by liquidating the common good. All calls to such a good, be it Liberty, Justice, or Equality, that Rousseau's *oeuvre* articulates have this polemical objective. They condemn and decry this absence: The human community is constitutively lacking; it can only *delinquere*, in both senses of the word. Yet community is what we need the most, as it is a part of our very selves: "Our sweetest existence is relative and collective, and our true *self* is not entirely within us."[5] Even the sustained declaration of his own solitude, upon which he almost obsessively insists in his final works, resounds with a silent revolt against the absence of community. Rousseau is alone because community does not exist, or, better, because all existent forms of community are nothing but the opposite of the only authentic one. In response, Rousseau protests against solitude as the negative imprint of an absolute need for sharing, which, however paradoxically, appears in his work as the written communication of his impossibility to communicate. Writing thus assumes the character of "solitude for others," of a "substitute for the human community that is unrealizable in social reality."[6]

Yet, as Emile Durkheim would point out, community is unrealizable from Rousseau's perspective because his critique of community lies within the same paradigm as Hobbesian individualism, wherein the individual is inscribed within his own completeness.[7] What is his "natural man" if not a monad, drawn to the other only by chance or misfortune? And does not the asocial—the only condition that Rousseau deems felicitous—plainly contradict his own aims for community? Because here is what condemns such an aim to failure: One cannot base a philosophy of community on a metaphysics of the individual. The presumed absoluteness of the individual cannot be put in common after the fact. Despite all of Rousseau's attempts, this antinomy cannot be resolved. The gap, both lexical and philosophical, between presupposition and result remains unbridgeable. When Rousseau attempts to represent community in a positive light, he risks imbuing community with the very untenable characteristics that have been highlighted by the harshest of his liberal critics. The point of distinction is located between the necessity for community to be present in a negative light in the critique of an existing society and its affirmative formulation. In other words, between the impolitical definition of the absence of community—community as an absence, a lack, an infinite debt with regard to the law that prescribes it—and its political realization.[8] To put it synthetically: Beginning with such metaphysical presuppositions—the individual enclosed in his own absoluteness—Rousseau's political community has potentially totalitarian leanings. By this I do not mean to refer to the specific category of twentieth-century "totalitarianism." Indeed, it's well known that Rousseau is always preoccupied with safeguarding the citizen from every abuse of state power, and that he uses the concept of "general will" precisely as an automatic corrective against any authoritarian tendency directed at the individual. As an integral part of the "general will," the individual is protected by the fact that all commands will have also been issued by him.[9]

Yet doesn't this kind of automatism—that is, the presupposed identification of each with all and of all with each—function as a totalizing mechanism that reduces the many to one? How else can one understand the well-known passage according to which "He who dares to undertake to give institutions to a nation ought to feel himself capable, as it were, of changing human nature; of transforming every individual, who in himself is a complete and independent whole, into part of a greater whole, from which he receives in some manner his life and his being"?[10] Here, it seems clear enough that the proto-totalitarian risk certainly won't be found in the contraposition of the communitarian and the individual models but in their superimposition, which traces community along the profile of the isolated and self-sufficient individual. The passage from the individual one to the collective one must run through a naturalistic channel. It's as if neither the individual nor the community can escape themselves; as if they do not know how to embrace the other without absorbing and incorporating him, without making him a part of themselves. Each time within Rousseau's work that such a project takes the form of a collective reality, which is to say a small homeland, city, or popular festival,[11] Rousseau's longing for community is overturned, becoming myth—the myth of a community that is transparent to itself, in which each member communicates to the other his communitarian ecstasy, his own dream of absolute self-immanence; a community without any mediation, filter, or sign that interrupts the reciprocal fusion of consciousnesses; without any distance, discontinuity, or difference from an other who is no longer such because he or she is an integral part of the one—the one that is lost, and found again, in his or her own identity.[12]

This myth of the unmediated community constitutes a risk that threatens Rousseau's discourse without crushing it. The author himself appears aware of it when he restrains himself from transposing this community of the heart onto a political community. And we, too, must be careful not to read *The Social Contract* as a political translation of the community of Clarens. Certainly, what is prefigured by the *Contract* is a democracy of affinity that excludes any distinction between the governors and the governed, between the legislative and the executive, between the people and the sovereign. Yet this is precisely why such a community is declared unrealizable, unless it's populated by gods: "Taking the term in its strict sense, there never existed, and never will exist, any true democracy."[13] And, if it were to exist, it would be the exact realization of its own opposite. Contrary to Rousseau's affirmation, but within his perspective, this conclusion wrests community from the grip of its myth. The antinomy refuses to resolve itself: Community is both necessary and impossible. Community not only offers itself in an ever-flawed way (insofar as it is never fully achieved) but is solely a *flawed* community, in the specific sense that what holds us together, what constitutes us as beings-in-common, as being-there-with [*conesserci*], is precisely that flaw, that nonfulfillment, that debt. In addition, it is our mortal finitude, as Rousseau himself foresaw in an unforgettable passage of *Émile*:

> It is man's weakness which makes him sociable; it is our common miseries which turn our hearts to humanity; we would owe humanity nothing if we were not men. . . . Men are not naturally kings, or lords, or courtiers, or rich men. All are born naked and poor; all are subject to the miseries of life, to sorrows, ills, needs, and pains of every kind. Finally, all are condemned to death. This is what truly belongs to man. This is what no mortal is exempt from.[14]

Kant seems to have arrived at a similar conclusion, consciously taking up the contradiction implicit in Rousseau and bringing it to its extreme consequences. It was no accident that Kant gave credit to Rousseau for having led him from the solitude of individual research to an interest in the common world of humankind.[15] Thought, more than anything else, requires community for its expression and development. Kant had said so in precisely these terms: "Yet how much and how correctly would we think if we did not think as it were in community with others to whom we communicate our thoughts, and who communicate theirs with us!"[16] It is not possible to think outside of the community—this is the Kantian presupposition that would be taken up in different ways by a series of interpreters and authors running from Lucien Goldmann to Hannah Arendt. If for Goldmann "the absolute and unrealizable necessity of reaching and actualizing totality constitutes the starting point of all of Kantian thought," for Arendt, sociability is not only the goal but also the origin of humanity, insofar as humankind essentially belongs to the world.[17] Kant's theory, continues Arendt, constitutes a rupture with respect to all others that subordinate dependence on kin to the sphere of needs and interests, as in utilitarian theories. Arguing against these, Kant asserts that judgment presupposes the existence of others, which is precisely why Arendt will take it up with regard to the field of action: "One judges always a member of a community, guided by one's community sense, one's *sensus communis*."[18] Community, therefore, is constitutive of our being human: Kant fully grasps, and consciously fulfills, Rousseau's intuition.

Yet the relationship between the two philosophers lies not only in their formulation of the necessity of community but, more fundamentally, in their shared consciousness of the absolutely problematic nature of community's realization. Even for Kant—actually, for him as for no other—community, as much as it is necessary, is impossible. The law prescribes what it interdicts, and it interdicts what it prescribes. This is why, as Goldmann also concludes, Kant lies at the origin of tragic thought, in radical contrast with the Hegelian-Marxist tradition. Still, contrary to what Goldmann and subsequent interpreters who took up and developed his point of view maintained, this not only doesn't place Kant in a sort of immature condition with respect to his dialectic successors (beginning as early as Fichte) but, on the contrary, shelters him from their totalizing tendency to historicize community in the state (Hegel), or against it (Marx).[19] Because herein lies the true legacy of Rousseau. Even Fichte, anticipating Marx, claims to "complete" Rousseau, but by saturating in mythopoetics the antinomy that Kant, vitally, holds open: If men are united by a universal form, they are irreparably separated by material contents and interests. The only way to realize community would be to overcome interests and individual differences, but interests and differences are in fact insurmountable, because they are also what constitute our nature. The tangible content is unable to be restored to the sphere of universality. Natural "sociability" is counterbalanced and contradicted by an equally natural "unsociability." This is why not only can community not *become* reality but it cannot even become a concept: It must, says the same law that demands it, remain a simple idea in reason, or an unrealizable goal, a pure destination.

Kant's assertion that "the sublime, yet never wholly attainable, idea of an ethical commonwealth dwindles markedly under men's hands" should be read as a continuation of Rousseau's formulation, cited above, about the unrealizability of true democracy.[20] Kant's reading is a continuation of Rousseau's, with the aggravating circumstance that, unlike Rousseau, for Kant, man is hunched by nature, so that the state of nature is, as it is for Hobbes, a state of war.[21] Bracketing for a moment Rousseau's positive reference to an origin in nature, this is what condemns the political condition to an incurable aporia. From this point of view, the problem of politics is clearly distinct from the problem of ethical ends. Politics cannot be thought in light of the good, just as praxis is different from theory. The ethical community could, completely hypothetically, "exist in the midst of a political community," but one differs from the other in principle, such that the political community cannot oblige its citizens to enter the ethical community without risking the ruin of both.[22] Certainly, Kant continues, it would be comforting to be able to imagine a likeness between the two, but to propose one would be reckless. As Lyotard might say, the ethical sentence can only be linked to the political sentence and to the cognitive one by the fragile bridge of *as if*.[23] But under that bridge runs an impossible abyss. The relationship between the political and ethical communities remains one of pure analogy: It can be expressed, like enthusiasm for the revolution, through symbols, signs, and emblems but not through historical proof or example, which instead regularly undermines it.[24] Politics can hope for the improvement of men and women, but politics may neither require nor necessarily foresee that improvement; politics must be potentially applicable also to a society of demons.[25] Politics is not a widening but a reduction of freedom, and such is a consequence, not a contradiction, of the absoluteness of freedom itself. This is precisely because the essence of freedom resides in its being unlimited, and the task of politics is to limit freedom with its opposite—an irresistible power.[26] It's no coincidence that Kant's state begins with force and coercion, even if, unlike in Hobbes, sovereignty must found itself on the rational principle, once again, however, *as if*—and *only as if*—it were based on the common will of the people.

This is the point that distances Kant from Rousseau. Freedom is intrinsically connected with evil: "The history of *nature* thus begins from good, for that is the *work of God*," writes Kant in a text dedicated to Rousseau; "the history of *freedom* begins from evil, for it is *the work of the human being*."[27] If human beings are born free, their origin can be nothing but evil. It's in this sense that guilt, that is, our *delinquere* as a lack of community toward which we are inclined and whence, though contradictorily, we come, is presupposed as the transcendental condition of our common humanity.[28] This is why, Kant writes, "man," instead of "ascribing his own misdeeds to an original crime of his ancestral parents . . . must recognize with full right what they did as having been done by himself and attribute the responsibility for all ills arising from the misuse of his reason entirely to himself."[29] Ernst Cassirer has already united Kant and Rousseau within such a semantics of guilt.[30] Now we need to take a step forward with regard to the degree of inevitability of such guilt. It is impossible to escape from guilt not simply because the temptation to break the law is irresistible but because law— that is, the categorical imperative—may not be put into practice, because it prescribes nothing but its own dutifulness; the law contains nothing but the formal obligation to obey it. We know that law requires only that we act in such a way that allows us to constitute our will on the principle of legislation for a universal community, but that the law in no way tells us what to do. On the contrary, it tells us that its injunctive strength resides precisely in what is not said. This is what is meant by the "categoricalness" of the imperative: on the one hand, its absolute, unconditional, and irrevocable sovereignty; on the other, its aprioristic withdrawal from any attempt at fulfillment. This imperative is therefore not only unfulfillable; it is the Unfulfillable itself.[31] This point should be outlined in particular detail. We cannot fulfill the law that enjoins us because law does not come from us. Law is in no way the self-legislation of the subject, because even the subject is subjected to law. The subject is subjected, however, only in the passive sense of "subjection," of "subjectification," rather than, for example, the more active sense of "subjectivity." On the contrary: Law corrodes, undermines, undoes our subjectivity. Law comes from the outside, and it leads us outside of ourselves. This is the case not only insofar as we cannot administer our own laws but also because of the more radical suggestion that law, as it unconditionally prescribes the unfulfillable, in a certain sense prescribes the destitution of the subject to whom it addresses itself. Law administers a statute of continual nonfulfillment. Law is an inextinguishable debt: "Whatever his state in the acquisition of a good disposition, and, indeed, however steadfastly a human being may have persevered in such a disposition in a life conduct conformable to it, *he nevertheless started from evil*, and this is a debt which is impossible for him to wipe out."[32] Law infinitely indebts the subject, which is not to say that law excludes the possibility of the subject. Kant in no way renounces the category of the "subject"; on the contrary, it's quite possible to say that he places it at the center of his system. It means, rather, that law includes the subject in his or her exteriority. Law insulates the subject from self-consistency. This is the case not only in the general sense that the subject's association with the law per se eliminates any subjective content—feelings, pleasure, interests—in favor of pure submission to a formal obligation. It is also the case in the more specific sense that the imperative may impose itself only by "harming," "damaging," or "humiliating" that irreducible nucleus of subjectivity that is constituted by "self-love" (*Selbstliebe*) or "amour propre" (*Eigenliebe*).[33]

Nevertheless, this reduction of the subject in the presence of and by the law impedes his or her fulfillment on one hand and on the other individuates an inside-out [*rovesciata*] and impolitical form of community characterized by nonfulfillment, defect, and finitude. Breaking the individual limits of the subject, those that Rousseau maintained intact, and thus emptying his or her anxiety for completion, law, in other words, *precisely insofar as it is unfulfillable* opens up for men and women another side of their being in common. What do human beings have in common? The impossibility to realize community, answers Kant. Or, put another way: their finite existence. Their being mortal. Their being "in time."

Toward the end of our itinerary we find Martin Heidegger. And yet it is to Heidegger that Kant owes his interpretation, which is focused more squarely on the theme of finitude. Even before the power [*potenza*] of the imperative, the Kantian subject is "finished" by his own temporal dimension.[34] Surely Kant does not yet grasp the innerworldly character of the subject in the Heideggerian sense of "being-in-the-world." Yet, displacing the subject from the aprioristic structure of temporality, Kant wrests from him every claim to completeness and commits him to a radically finite figure. Upon this figure is grafted the thematic of law, which follows a circular route of cause and effect: Because he or she is structurally finite, the subject is subjugated to law, but it is the subjection to law that renders him or her constitutively finite. "A creature that is fundamentally interested in a duty knows itself in a not-yet-having-fulfilled, so that what indeed it should do becomes questionable to it. This not-yet of a fulfilling, which is itself still undetermined, gives us a clue that a creature whose innermost interest is with a duty is fundamentally finite."[35] Here, through Kant, Heidegger means not simply that the nonfulfillment of a duty determines a situation of finitude but instead that finitude ultimately coincides with that duty. Heidegger means that we cannot not be finite in the imperative sense that we *must* be finite. We are obliged to examine the issue from both sides: We are finite because we cannot fulfill the law, and therefore law is something that transcends us continually. Such transcendence, from another point of view, is nothing but the limit of our possibility of fulfilling the law, and therefore the index and the measure of our finitude.

Law, in other words, comes from an elsewhere that is nevertheless within us, that constitutes us as "subjects," but only to law itself. Heidegger expresses this in *Being and Time* in the formula "The call comes *from* me, and yet *over* me."[36] With this, Heidegger has already taken a path that, pushing Kant's transcendentalism to its extreme consequences, ends up translating it into a different vocabulary—namely, that of the analytic of existence. What the two philosophers retain in common, in spite of what appears to be a change in conceptual and linguistic frames, is, on the one hand, the presupposed character of guilt with respect to the definition of moral good and evil: It is not the option of evil which determines our fall into guilt because one cannot "fall" into guilt if it is from this that one originates. On the contrary, guilt is what makes evil possible. On the other hand, there is the necessity that one take "care" of such presupposed guiltiness (*Schuldigsein*), which is the same thing, given that "care" (*Sorge*) means "being guilty."[37] Yet, while for Kant the "taking care" of originary guiltiness consists of a commitment to the realization of given values or compliance with given norms that is destined to fail, for Heidegger it means nothing but the simple acknowledgement of the nullity of the self's own foundation. This is why, as we have seen in Kant, guilt cannot be abolished but must "decide," however defectively, to "take care." This is why the "call" affirms nothing but rather speaks through silence. Certainly, as we have seen, even in Kant the law prescribes only its binding categoricalness, but this always occurs within a lexicon that is prescriptive, in which something is recommended. In Heidegger, along with prescription every realizing impulse falls away, even if it were to pertain to the unrealizable. In short, while for Kant it is still possible and, indeed, utterly necessary to speak of an ethics, however "finite," in Heidegger finitude is the only declension of ethics, in the radical sense of that which signals its "end."

This stalemate assumes full visibility in relation to the question of community. We have seen how the constitution of community is the most fundamental objective of Kantiansm, even if it is destined to an inevitable stalemate. Community is both that toward which all efforts of men and women who deserve to be called as such are oriented and also that which, given their natural unsociability, they will never be able to fully realize. The reason for such a contradiction is related to the fact that, as with Rousseau, Kant cannot draw a communal outcome from an individualistic anthropology. With regard to Rousseau's naturalism, Kant effects such a radical deconstruction of natural origins that he denies them of every affirmative qualification. Still, natural origins remain, however negatively, within a horizon that is anthropological. Indeed, it is actually this negativity or unsociability, in psychological terms, that bars the law of universal community and prohibits its realization. Heidegger poses the question quite differently. For him, community, at least as Kant understands it—that is, as a universal ethics—is not realizable. What in Kantianism is posed in terms of an unfulfillable project in Heidegger takes on the character of a destiny. Such a shift excludes every ethical semantics: The loss of community occurs not because of men and women's failed attempt to create community; instead, loss is the situation from which community comes. For this reason, every hypothesis of a "fall" misses the mark. Da-sein [*l'esserci*] cannot "fall" because it "has initially always already fallen away from itself and fallen prey to the 'world,'" so that we might say that it "plunges out of itself into itself."[38] If this is so, however, it means that the fall constitutes the very origin of Da-sein. It therefore also means that all the authors who from Rousseau onward attempted, in vain, to found community by reconstructing its originary logical conditions fail not because the conditions have forever vanished into an entropic vortex but because the conditions themselves are nothing but that very vortex. This in turn means that community is not realizable—if we want to continue to use such inadequate terminology—only because community is always already realized, in the sense that it is that very "defect" contemplated instead from the vantage point of its original destinality [*destinalità*]. From this vantage point, any effort to arrive at an end is no less useless than attempting to rediscover an origin. Community is situated neither before nor after society. It is neither that which society has destroyed (following the nostalgic readings à la Ferdinand Tönnies) nor the objective that society must set for itself (following instead the utopian readings of Marxian extraction)—just as it is not the result of a pact, of a will, or of a simple necessity shared by individuals. Nor is it the archaic locus whence individuals originate and that they have abandoned: this for the simple reason that individuals, insofar as they are individuals and aside from their being-in-a-common-world-with-others, do not exist. "On the basis of this *like-with* being-in-the-world, the world is always already the one that I share with the others. The world of Da-sein is a *with-world*. Being-in is *being-with* others. The innerworldly being-in-itself of others is *Mitda-sein*."[39] This is also true when the other is not present or known, since even being alone, which is the transcendental condition of Rousseau's originary man, is a figure that is can be determined only negatively, and only in its relation to the common. Bear in mind, however, that we may in no way deduce from this that community is fulfilled, immanent to itself, or that it coincides with its own meaning. Even Heidegger risked thinking as much, not only at the beginning of the 1930s but already in *Being and Time*, when he was tempted to historicize the "community of destiny" of a single people.[40] On the contrary: community, as we have already noted, not only always offers itself in a defective way but is only a community insofar as it is constituted by a defect. What holds us in common, or, better, what establishes us as beings-in-common, being-there-with [*con-esserci*], is that defect, that nonfulfillment, that debt. But also our mortal finitude. This is revealed not so much in that our relationship with others is thought in terms of being-toward-death, but instead the specific modality that this relationship assumes, or what we have already noted as a reciprocal "care." Care, rather than interest, lies at the basis of community. Community is determined by care, and care by community. One may not exist without the other: "care-in-common." Yet, and here is the novelty of Heidegger's analytic, this means that the duty of community (providing, yet not conceding, that there is one) is not to liberate us from care but instead to protect it as the sole thing that renders community possible. This specification takes into account Heidegger's distinction between two distinct, and opposing, modalities of "taking care" of the other. The first is a substitution of oneself for him, taking his place so as to liberate him from care. The second is to urge him toward it, to liberate him not from but *toward* his cure (*Fürsorge*): "This concern which essentially pertains to authentic care; that is, the existence of the other, and not to a *what* which takes care of it, helps the other to become more transparent to himself *in* his care and *free for* it."[41] This means that the figure of the Other ultimately coincides with that of community. At the same time this is so not in the obvious sense in which every one of us has something to do with the other but rather in the sense that the other constitutes us from deep within. It's not that we communicate with the other but that we *are* the other. To paraphrase Rimbaud, we are nothing other from the other.[42] Or, we are strangers to ourselves, as has been claimed countless times. The point is: How do we translate this formula into the reality of our subjectivity? How do we "convince" our obstinate identity? And once again, community presents us with its enigma: impossible and necessary. Necessary and impossible. We are still far from having fully thought it through.

MELANCHOLY AND COMMUNITY

What kind of relationship exists between these two terms? Is there something essentially "common" in melancholy, and does melancholy have something to do with the very form of community? The answer that the literature on melancholy has offered has often been negative. Within both its pathological interpretation as a sickness of the body and spirit and its positive one as genial exceptionality, melancholy has generally been situated as not only different from community but actually in opposition to it. Indeed, we might say that for much of the interpretative tradition, and most markedly within sociological inquiry, melancholic man has been defined precisely by his opposition to communal life. He has been defined insofar as he is *not* in common: sick, abnormal, even ingenious, but, because of this, outside of the community, if not against it. He may resemble a beast or a god (following the classic Aristotelian definition) but resembles neither humankind in general nor the common generality of men. In fact, no matter how widespread, recurring, and proliferated in an infinite variety of cases and typologies—and no matter how much it is applied to a growing number of individuals—melancholy has always been understood and treated as if it were an individual phenomenon. Only an individual or individuals can be melancholic. Society may not be so, insofar as one of the primary characteristics of melancholy is asociality, isolation, and the refusal of collective life. In its operative and productive intention, in its compulsion toward order and rationality, this collective life is in turn interpreted as that which does not tolerate melancholy within it, to the point that collective life must liberate itself from melancholy through expulsion, repression, or therapeutic inclusion. The oppositional schema remains, as melancholy and community are thought of in the form of a reciprocal repugnance. Where one exists, the other may not. They are not only factually but also conceptually incompatible.

But is this actually the case? Is it really true that melancholy is confined to the outside of community, or at least to its most blind corners, in the unproductive and irrational zones that community carries within itself as residues that are every so often expelled from or fully conquered by collective life? In truth, the great modern philosophical tradition, like the great iconological and literary traditions before it, radically contested this simplified and superficial reading, ultimately overturning its fundamental presupposition and producing a no less problematic image: A figure that is itself melancholic, turned in upon itself self-critically and thereby proving that melancholy, is not, nor can it be, a simple object of analysis but something—a power [*potenza*], magnet, or abyss that tends irresistibly to capture and suck in the very subject who analyzes. Actually, true philosophy has always grasped not only the "common" character of melancholy throughout a long line of well-known interpretation that runs from the church fathers to Heidegger but also, and more importantly, the originary melancholic, lacerated, and fractured character of community. That tradition has always grasped that melancholy is not an occasional illness, a contingent character, or even a simple content of community but instead something that concerns community much more fundamentally, to the point of constituting its very form. Melancholy is not something that community contains along with other attitudes, postures, or possibilities but something by which community itself is contained and determined. Or better, melancholy is something by which community is "decided": something that cuts and discards community within itself, constituting it precisely in the form of that cut or that refuse. Melancholy resembles a fault and a wound that community experiences not as a temporary or partial condition but as community's only way of being; and of not being, or of being precisely in the form of its own "not," but of that which must be, but that cannot be, if not in a defective, negative, concave modality. This is the modality of absence to oneself that Jacques Lacan defined as "lack of being" (*manque à être*) or "pure lack" (*pure manque*).

Here, in this initial separating, in this splitting of the very Beginning, lies melancholy: not *in* community, and not even *of* community, but *as* community—as an originary gap that separates the existence of the community from its own essence. Melancholy is like an unbreakable wall [*limite*] that community hurls itself against and bounces back from, unable to cross. Or melancholy is like the Thing, *la chose* or *das Ding*, that is impossible to realize because, like the Thing, melancholy is made of nothing and impossible to appropriate because melancholy is made up of expropriation itself. What else is community if not the lack of "one's own"? What is it if not *not* one's own and that which is unable to be appropriated? This is the meaning that is etymologically inscribed within the very *munus* from which *communitas* is derived and that it carries within itself as its own nonbelonging to itself, as a not belonging, or an impropriety, of all the members that make up community through a reciprocal distortion, which is the distortion of community itself: Its always being different from what it wants to be, its not being able to exist as such, its impossibility of becoming a common undertaking without destroying itself—herein lies the meaning and the root of our common melancholy. If community is nothing but the relation— the "with" or the "between"—that joins multiple subjects, this means that it cannot be a subject, individual or collective. Community is not an "entity" [*ente*] but instead a "non-entity" [*un ni-ente*], a non-being [*non-ente*] that precedes and cuts every subject, wresting him or her from identification with him or herself and submitting him or her to an irreducible alterity.

From this point of view, which does not merely inquire after the encounter between community and melancholy but instead interrogates their aporetic intersection, every facile analogy between *communitas* and *res publica* is cast in doubt. Community is not a *res*, and it is certainly not the *Res*. It is not the Thing but its lack. It is the opening from which our *cum* bursts forth and into which our *cum* continues to slide. If we fail to grasp this constitutive and imperative link between thing and nothing, which melancholy at once undergoes and safeguards, we risk being stuck with a reductive and simplified image of community. Or, worse, we risk forcing community open until we make it explode, or implode, with catastrophic effects. This is what melancholy has always taught us: The limit may not be eliminated, the Thing is not entirely within our reach, community is not identifiable with itself, with all of itself and with itself as all, if not in a form that is unequivocally totalitarian. What was twentieth-century totalitarianism if not the illusion, the furious illusion, of being able to identify community with itself and, in so doing, to fulfill it? What was totalitarianism if not the phantasmatic temptation of abolishing the limit, of filling in the fault, of closing the wound, if not the criminal presumption that community might be definitively healed of its melancholy, or the illusion that we could immunize ourselves from the disease of melancholy by destroying its carrier germs, found perhaps in the flesh of the melancholy people *par excellence*, without realizing that trying to liberate the thing from its nothing means obliterating the thing itself?

We did not need to wait for modern philosophy to grasp the tight knot that binds the common thing and nothing, or the constitutively melancholy character of community. Indeed, to what else do all the narratives about founding offenses from Cain to Romulus refer if not precisely to a *delin-quere* (in the Latin sense of "lack") from which society is born and that it inevitably carries within itself? What do these narratives mean, once stripped of their mythical significance as victimized sacrifice, if not the trauma, breach, or lacuna carved in the very body of the community from the beginning? The one who theorized what in classical mythology is simply a melancholy tonality is Thomas Hobbes, when he translated the *delinquere* of founding myths into the terribly literal form of an infraspecific offense placed at the origin of the human community. Even more than in the pages dedicated specifically to melancholy—*madness, dejection,* and *grief,* but also explicitly *melancholy* [in English], as it is defined in the *Leviathan*—it is in the presupposition of a generalized capacity for killing as the originary form of the human relationship that marks the structurally melancholy character of Hobbes's political theory. For Hobbes, melancholy is not only one of the destructive passions that, if left unchecked, risks leading men into civil war. This is what defines melancholy, rather than as an individual pathology, as a sickness of the *political body* [in English] in its entirety. Upon further consideration, it also reveals itself as the very structure of a social existence that is entirely confined to the political trade-off between two fears: a reciprocal fear of each man toward the other and a fear that must push the state itself to impede the destructive proliferation of the first fear. In this way, what takes shape is a double melancholy or a folding in of melancholy on itself, which is to say a melancholy of both cause and remedy, natural state and civil state, an originary violence and a derivative one. It is not by chance that the political order—that is, the institution of the state—is founded on the subjects' renouncing of every power and turning it over to one who, in order to defend their lives, is also authorized to kill them.

The melancholy, if not mournful, character of such a situation is best expressed in Freud's *Totem and Taboo,* through the myth that seems to retrace the sacrificial logic of the Hobbesian paradigm down to the detail. Not only is the constitutive act of community found in the assassination of the father by the brothers but such an act is sanctioned by the double renouncement necessary for the establishment of civil order: a renouncing of women, whose fault it is that the brothers killed the father, and a renouncing of their own identities, produced through the embodiment of their dead father and their identification with his figure. Here the melancholy characterization of the "many"—precisely those murderous brothers so often optimistically interpreted as the free citizens of democracy—assumes perhaps its most radical form: The subjects of modern politics may constitute themselves as such only by taking the place of the ancient sovereign that they killed. Yet, in devouring his body, they incorporate his very death. They can only assume power by dying themselves as subjects, by submitting themselves to death. Here is the true reason for the feeling of guilt that they carry within: not only the murder of the father but the interiorized assumption of his death. This is the extreme form of political melancholy: sacrificing the father first and the brothers to the sacrificed father next. A double sacrifice, sacrifice squared. Blood and inhibition, inhibition and blood. We, declare the brothers, are the Sovereign, the Community, and the State. But we are such only insofar as we have always belonged and will always belong to the death that we once gave and ate. We are what we never were and what we may no longer be: We were the other whom we expelled for good and who will always return within us. What else does the famous image of the *Leviathan*, composed of so many figures embedded within each other, signify if not the reciprocal incorporation of the dead father within the sons and the sons in the dead father? Was this not the darkest essence of melancholy that was portrayed in Saturn, who devoured his own sons before they could castrate him?

One might say that all great political thought contains this image of guilt and perdition, even among those, beginning with Rousseau, who contested most vehemently Hobbes's sacrificial logic. Certainly, with regard to Hobbes, everything appears overturned in both intention and outcome except the fundamental presupposition that politics is marked by an originary guilt— that is, by a defect, debt, or wound that it has historically never been able to heal because history itself carries the originary guilt as it tries to detach from its own nonhistorical origin. Here, with respect to Hobbes's sacrificial model, melancholy, the sickness of "many," refers not so much to the lacerated character of the origin as much as to the irreversible detachment that wrests us from it. Next, we have the melancholy of the Rousseau's man, separated from his own presupposition and held in contradiction with it, much like he who may not be what he should be. This is the melancholy of an existence that has lost its own essence and of an essence that can no longer find a way to become an existence. In Rousseau, the fracture of melancholy cuts across the entire horizon of history. History depicts itself as an uninterrupted stratum of melancholy. This community is no longer the Hobbesian one of the offense, but it is one that is impossible to realize. Here lies community's unsolvable melancholy: Community is only definable on the basis of the lack from which it is derived and that connotes community as an absence, or a defect, of community. It is only interpretable as an impossibility, as that which it is not and that which it may never be, just as nature is only recognizable through its necessary denaturalization, within the cone of shade that its own opposite projects upon it. Rousseau's oeuvre, including his autobiographical texts, which signal the all-time apex of melancholic literature, is legible as a yearning nostalgia for the absent community. Even the sustained declaration, above all in his last writings, of his own solitude bears the negative imprint of an absolute need for sharing. Jean-Jacques is alone because no true community exists, because all existing communities are but a negation of themselves. His very writing assumes the melancholy character of "solitude for others." It is, in an extreme paradox, the communication of its own impossibility to communicate. It is the dissatisfied claiming of a "commonplace" that is recognizable only upon its removal—in its own absolute fragility. As Rousseau writes in *Èmile*:

> Men are not naturally kings, or lords, or courtiers, or rich men. All men are born naked and poor; all are subject to the miseries of life, to sorrows, ills, needs, and pains of every kind. Finally, all are condemned to death. This is what truly belongs to man. This is what no mortal is exempt from.[1]

Nevertheless, we are warned of something already in this passage: a tone or an accent that begins to break down the radically negative frame within which we have been defining the relationship between community and melancholy. It is true that community is itself removed from every possibility of fulfillment, that it only offers itself in the form of lack and defect. At the same time, that defect, that limit, however, is also understood as something that unites men in a common destiny—namely, that of their own finitude. In reality, it's Kant who will accomplish such a conceptual shift, not toward a less melancholic reading of community but toward a more articulate and open interpretation of melancholy. Within modern philosophy, it's Kant who initiates a turning of the concept of melancholy on itself whose effects are not fully understood even today but in whose shock wave we move about without knowing exactly where we are being pushed. This is so not because in Kant a tragic, dark, mournful note of Pietistic-Lutheran extraction still reverberates that communicates the irresolvable defect of human nature, the metaphor of the "crooked timber of humanity" that no rational law will be able to straighten out. Nor is this because his oeuvre lacks a vocabulary of "guilt" and "radical evil" as an element that sinisterly characterizes the entire sphere of action and man's very being. On the contrary, from this angle Kant's position is even more desperate than Rousseau's because it lacks every positive mythology of natural origin. Kantian philosophy prescribes no return to the natural origin of man because such an origin harbors a radically negative seed. This is why Kant's man has no dreams of reappropriating his own essence (though for Rousseau, as, in a certain way, for Marx, he still does), because that essence has been marked since the beginning by a feature that disfigures it irreparably. Thus it is no longer possible to say, as Rousseau does, that man's natural origin has been degraded in history; instead, history has fallen—that is, has been flung into the originary fissure. Within man's origin, says Kant, already lies that freedom that implicitly carries the possibility of evil.

Herein lies the linchpin of Kant's discourse, which is destined to rewrite in affirmative terms his very definition of melancholy. If freedom carries within it the possibility of evil, this also means that the possibility of evil always relies on an act of freedom, that it can always turn itself into good. It is to freedom—that is, to its profoundly contradictory character—that Kant links the essence of melancholy. As we know, Kant focuses on the melancholy temperament primarily in his essay on beauty and the sublime. In that essay, melancholy is uniquely tied to what Kant understands as the sublime—that is, that affect born from the feeling of inadequateness when confronted with the imagination's task to adapt to reason. Melancholy is linked to that impulse which, aspiring to boundlessness, experiences the infrangibility of limits. Like the sublime, melancholy is the traumatic experience of limits, of the inclination to overcome them and the impossibility of doing so. This melancholic dialectic is related to the very nature of Kantian law, which is characterized by a constitutive antinomy. The law, the categorical imperative, can never be carried out, not only because of man's irresistible inclination to break it but, even more profoundly, because the categorical imperative does not prescribe anything but his dutifulness—no content beyond the formal obligation of obedience. For this reason, the categorical imperative is thus not only unfulfillable but is The Unfulfillable itself. The categorical imperative prescribes those it addresses a statute of perennial nonfulfillment. Here is what causes the melancholy of the Kantian subject but also the awareness of his own limits that melancholy restores to him. For this reason, Kant concludes, melancholy is akin to a virtue that surpasses its generic Aristotelian and Ficinian link with genius. Melancholy is a virtue for Kant because, wresting man from every unmerited self-valorization, it procures for him that moral consciousness that is inseparable from his own freedom. Continuously striking against his own insuperable limits, the melancholic man is the only one who grasps that the only way to realize a lack is to keep it as such. The Thing is inseparable from nothing. The Real—"the thing per se"—is incapable of being appropriated. Kant's melancholic man knows that community as such is unrealizable, that the *munus* of our *communitas* is the law that prohibits its perfect fulfillment. Yet perhaps Kant's melancholic man is also the first to know that that *munus* is also a gift, that that impossibility which reminds men of their finitude also endows them with the freedom of to choose that it may become its necessary opposite.

At the end of this itinerary opened up by Kant—and, that is, at the beginning of a new melancholic thought that is no longer translatable into a melancholy *of* thought but instead one that allows thought the strength and courage to rid itself of every melancholic tone—we encounter, naturally, Heidegger. It's as if the entire history of the philosophy, literature, and iconology of melancholy had found in Heidegger's thought a place to converge and overflow. It's as if that history intensified to the point of incandescence and combustion until it caught fire and assumed a new form. Already in *Being and Time*, indeed, Heidegger grasps both declinations of melancholy: the negative one, meaning *tristitia* or *acedia*, and the positive one, meaning the profound consciousness of finitude. He situates the first in the sphere of the inauthentic, or improper, and the second in the sphere of authentic and proper existence. In the first case, melancholy (*Schwermut*) is the habit of moving from one desire to another without satisfying either and therefore enduring one's own limits as an obstacle and a constraint. In the second case, melancholy is related to that *Angst* that suits not depression but the "calm" and also the "joy" of accepting the limit, or finitude, as the condition that belongs most properly to us.

What counts even more and what becomes increasingly clear beginning with the so-called Heideggerian turn of the 1930s, is that this double phenomenology of melancholy does not translate two different and opposing possibilities of the human experience, even though the two faces are always linked—since the authentic is nothing but the mature awareness of our originary inauthenticity, just as the proper is the conscious acceptance of our originary inauthenticity. It is from this perspective, which Heidegger of course does not always place in the foreground and more than once actually distorts and betrays, that melancholy is again reformulated. Melancholy is meant no longer or not only as an abnormal or ingenious attitude but as something that has to do with the very form of thought: "All creative action resides in a mood of melancholy [*Schwermut*], whether we are clearly aware of the fact or not, whether we speak at length about it or not."[2] How should we interpret Heidegger's statement? In what way does melancholy touch philosophy to the point of coinciding completely with it? Certainly, responding adequately to this question would imply already having grasped, in its fullest extent and intensity, and then crossed the margin that, instead, we still inhabit. It would mean already occupying the opening that the closure of the metaphysical horizon discloses at its outer limits. It would mean grasping this new sense, free from the complete exhaustion of every meaning that our incurably hermeneutic civilization has always presupposed and imposed on the originary indeterminacy of meaning.

All of this is still quite far from possible, and belongs to a time that has yet to come. And nevertheless it is possible to say something about it, beginning with the outermost edge of Heidegger's philosophy: something that once again has to do with the question of community. To propose that melancholy coincides with the very essence of thought when there is no opposition between the authentic and the inauthentic, that our most proper dimension is precisely in the consciousness of our essential impropriety, or that we have no essence but simple existence—all of this means that incompleteness, finitude, is not the limit of community, as the melancholy strand of thought has always imagined, but instead its very meaning. This is why Heidegger can write not only that "being-alone is a deficient mode of being-with" but also that "its possibility is a proof for the latter."[3] Because community is not, as Rousseau claimed, something to which we must return, nor is it, as Kant claimed, something to which we must aspire. Nor is it, as Hobbes thought, something to destroy, something destructible. Community is neither an origin nor a *telos*. Community is neither a goal nor an end, neither a presupposition nor a destination, but the condition, both singular and plural, of our complete existence. It is here, which is to say in this acceptance of the limit not as a liminal space to endure or break but as the only common place for which we've been destined, as the originary *munus* that unites us, that melancholic thought touches a point beyond which we don't yet know where to go. Yet it is from this very point that the ancient name *melancholia* will correspond to a meaning quite different from all those that the philosophical tradition has thus far assigned it.

IMMUNITARY DEMOCRACY

Does the term *community* refer to democracy? Might it, or is it too profoundly rooted in the conceptual lexicon of the romantic, authoritarian, and racist Right? This question, first posed in the context of American neo-communitarianism, is emerging once again in Europe, above all in France and Italy, as we venture a new thought about community. This question is not only legitimate but in certain ways quite unavoidable at a time when democratic culture is interrogating its own theoretical mandates and its own future. However, this doesn't change the fact that the question is incorrect in its very formulation, or in any case poorly articulated because, as it seeks to situate community, the question assumes a concept (democracy) as an indicator and a term of comparison that is entirely incapable of "comprehending" community.[1] This is so not only because democracy, at least in its modern meaning, is incomparably newer than community; as a concept, democracy is also flatter, and increasingly crammed into an entirely political-institutional casing.

Whereas the politico-logical notion of democracy carries a deficit of depth and substance, community carries, quite differently, a semantic richness, not only on the vertical plane of history but also on the synchronic plane of meaning. This is not the place to attempt a comprehensive reconstruction of community. My recent research on the Latin etymology of *communitas* and the older term *munus* from which it is derived, constitutes an initial examination of the historical and semantic richness of the concept.[2] With regard to our opening query, we can deduce that the correct question isn't whether community might reenter the lexicon of democracy but rather whether democracy can reenter, or at least acquire some of its own meaning within the lexicon of community. Without attempting an immediate response, we should bring the term *community* into sharper focus. In so doing, the conceptual dichotomies with which twentieth-century philosophy attempted to define community will be of no help, as they overlooked the originary meaning of community. I'm referring not only to the community built by the so-called (American) communitarians against their alleged adversaries the liberals. Such communities instead constitute the interface between communitarians and liberals, insofar as the former unwittingly shares the same subjectivist and individualistic lexicon as the latter, only they apply it to community itself rather than to the individual, or to the community as many distinct individuals who are opposed to one another. I'm also referring to the entrenched opposition between "community" and "society" that reached the zenith of its typological ordering in Ferdinand Tönnies's *Community and Civil Society (Gemeinschaft und Gesellschaft)*.[3] I say this because even this formulation of community, however more philosophically apt than the first, resides entirely within one of the two ostensibly contrasting terms, in this case *society*, such that community is entirely produced by society. This idea of community is not only born from modern society; society only assumes meaning in contrast to community. It is *Gesellschaft* [society] that "constructs" its own ideal-typical opposite so that society can found itself, in apologetic or denigrating terms, depending upon the vantage point from which one observes and judges it. The fact that the organic *Gemeinschaft* [community] that Tönnies and his many (and less shrewd) twentieth-century imitators discuss never existed as such is both the sign and the confirmation of the mythological character of the dichotomy that founds community. Community is nothing but a figure of society in its most fully developed self-interpretation, which coincides with society's incipient crisis.

Does this mean that we may not say anything about community, that it has no logical or historical opposite capable of defining it categorically? As I've attempted to demonstrate, this isn't exactly the case; only it would require us to return to a meaning of community that has the same diachronic depth and the same semantic power of the concept to which it refers by way of contrast. Rather than being opposed artificially, from the outside, as happens with the modern ideas of "individual," "society," or "freedom" [*libertà*], community corresponds with its opposite in a kind of originary co-belonging. It's this meaning of community that I attempted to uncover in the idea of "immunization," derived from the Latin term *immunitas* and linked precisely to *communitas* through the relationship (in the first case negative and in the second case positive) to the *munus*. If the members of the *communitas* are bound by the same law, by the same duty, or gift to give (the meanings of *munus*), *immunis* is he or she who is exempt or exonerated from these. *Immunis* is he or she who has no obligations toward the other and can therefore conserve his or her own essence in tact as a subject and owner of himself or herself.[4] What are the advantages of this etymological-paradigmatic choice? First and foremost, the perfect co-implication of these two concepts excludes them from being laid out along a line of historical succession wherein one follows the other and replaces it following the optimistic or pessimistic procedures of any philosophy of history: the individual, society, or freedom, who would overcome, or lose—according to the "progressive" or "regressive" inclination of its interpreter—the ancient community. Another advantage would be the fact that such a choice opens a larger horizon of visibility for democracy, which I understand not only in a politicological key but also and above all in a socioanthropological one. If there is something that remains lacking in the endless contemporary debate about democracy, it is this deep scrutiny of the constitution of *homo democraticus* that Tocqueville inaugurated with an unparalleled intensity.[5]

Yet the category of "immunization" is capable of restoring to the analysis of democracy the same kind of analytical richness and interdisciplinary mobility with which the great social philosophy of the 1930s and 1950s investigated the anthropology of *homo totalitarius* (here I refer not only to the Frankfurt school but also to the work of the Parisian *Collège de sociologie*, and in particular to Bataille's great essay on fascism).[6] From this angle, the profound relationship that links community and democracy in a single aporetic knot comes into full view. Modern democracy speaks a language that is opposed to that of community insofar as it always has introjected into it an immunitary imperative.

It was already clear to the great twentieth-century tradition of negative anthropology—from Helmuth Plessner to Arnold Gehlen and Niklas Luhmann, through the systemic reconversion of the "Hobbesian paradigm of order" undertaken by Parsons—that the category of immunization, in its head-on confrontation with that of community, was the most fruitful interpretative key for modern political systems. In an essay entitled *The Limits of Community*, Plessner juxtaposes community with the immunitary logic of the "democratic game."[7] In a world in which individuals who are naturally at risk confront one another in a competition whose stakes are power and prestige, the only way to avoid a catastrophic outcome is to institute among them sufficient distance so as to immunize each from everyone else. Against every communitarian temptation, the public sphere is where men and women enter into relation in the form of their disassociation. From here the need arises for strategies and control apparatuses that allow men and women to live next to one another without touching, and therefore to enlarge the sphere of individual self-sufficiency by using "masks" or "armor" that defend them from undesired and insidious contact with the other. As Elias Canetti also reminds us, nothing scares the individual more than being touched by what threatens to cross his or her individual boundaries.[8] In this anthropological frame—dominated as it is by the principle of fear and the persistence of insecurity—politics itself ends up resembling an art of diplomacy that conceals a relationship of natural enmity in courteous forms of etiquette, tact, and civil behavior.

What in Plessner's work maintains a directive that oscillates between art and technology assumes in Gehlen's work a decidedly institutional character. Gehlen also begins with Hobbes's (and Nietzsche's) observation about the natural lack of man with regard to other animal species and the need to transform this biological lack into a life-preserving possibility.[9] Unlike his predecessor, however, Gehlen is careful to root this immunitary option in an actual theory of institutions.[10] In a situation of excessive environmental impact and pressures, institutions are charged with exonerating man from the weight with which the contingency of events saddles him. This requires a kind of "plasticity," or a capacity to adapt to a given situation so as not to expose the individual to an unbearable conflict. It also requires a mastery of one's own instincts that inhibits them from being dissolved and instead channels them in a self-reproducing way, in the same way in which the satisfaction of needs is contained and deferred in a rigidly controlled frame of compatibility. Only through this double renunciation can men and women immunize themselves permanently from the dangers presented by their own lacking structure—that is, by filling in that initial void that removes them from themselves and re-appropriating what is not naturally theirs. Yet filling that void, making proper what is not one's own, is equivalent to reducing the "common" to the point of extinction. Indeed, the exoneration from environmental contingency that institutions ensure coincides, for the democratic subject, with a taking of distance from the world in which he or she is rooted, and, for this very reason, with a relieving of that common *munus* that obligates him with regard to others. In this way, he or she is compelled to close his originary openness, and to circumscribe him or herself within his or her own interior. What is immunization if not a kind of progressive interiorization of exteriority? If community is our "outside" [*fuori*], the outside-of-us, immunization is what brings us back within ourselves by severing all contact with the outside [*esterno*].

Niklas Luhmann was certainly the one who carried this logic to its extreme consequences. Situated at the intersection of Parsons's functionalism and the regulatory paradigm of cybernetic models, his theory constitutes the most refined articulation of immunitary logic as a specific form of modernization. Moreover, he writes, "certain historical tendencies stand out, indicating that since the early modern period, and especially since the eighteenth century, endeavors to secure a social immunology have intensified."[11] He also writes that the immunitary system that originally coincided with law was extended to all spheres of social life, from economics to politics. We see such a tendency in Luhmann's seminal definition of the relationship between system and environment. There the problem of systemically controlling dangerous environmental conflicts is resolved not only through a simple reduction of environmental complexity but instead through its transformation from exterior complexity to a complexity that is internal to the system itself. To this first strategy of interiorization, however, which is activated by an immunitary process, a second is added which is much more laden with consequences for environmental difference—namely, its complete inclusion within the system or its objective elimination. This development in Luhmann's thought, which occurs when he adopts the biological concept of autopoiesis, shifts the lens from the defensive level of the systemic government of the environment to an internal self-regulation of systems that is completely independent and autonomous with regard to environmental pressures. The system reproduces itself in increasingly complex forms, such that it constitutes the very elements that compose it. Clearly, this perfectly circular logic has the effect not only of breaking any possible relationships with the outside but also of calling into question the very idea of "outside." If the contradictions that ensnare democratic systems ultimately have the function of alerting their immunitary apparatus in order to stimulate a defensive reaction against any threat of destruction, it means that these contradictions no longer place the outside in contrast with the inside. They are nothing but the outside *of* the inside, merely one of its folds. This also means that the immunitary system "immunized" such a communication by including it in its referential mechanism. It means that the entire communicative flow is nothing but the self-reproductive projection of the immunizing process: "The immune system disposes over the use of 'no,' of communicative rejection. It operates *without communication with the environment.*"[12]

If we compare these passages of Luhmann's immunitary theory with the history of immunology as an ever more important branch of biomedicine, the connections are remarkable. We know that the object of immunology is the capacity of vertebrates to react to the introduction of extraneous substances by producing antibodies that are capable of defending their biochemical identity. In systemic terms, this means responding adequately to the challenges of the environment represented by external antigens. Yet with the passage from chemical immunology to molecular immunology, this general frame undergoes profound changes that head in the same direction as those attempted by systems theory: from defense with regard to the outside to internal self-regulation. The crux of the question regards the role of the antigen (the virus received from the outside) in producing the antibody. How is the reaction of the antibody linked to the action of the antigen? The response that gained ground beginning in the middle of the twentieth century, beginning with the work of Paul Erlich and continuing through that of Niels Kaj Jerne, is that the immunitary antibody is not determined by the introduction of the antigen but rather preexists it. Without recapitulating even the most salient points of this long and controversial debate (for this, Albert I. Tauber's work is instructive), what matters for our discussion is that in Luhmann's theory as in new molecular immunology, the central problem is no longer the capacity of the organism to distinguish his own components from extraneous ones but the internal self-regulation of the immunitary system itself.[13] If antibody cells transmit even in the absence of antigens (or external stimuli), the immune system assumes the characteristics of a web of internal identifications that are entirely self-sufficient. This is the final outcome of the immunitary war that has been waged since the advent of modernity against risks of communal "infection." To say that there is no longer an outside against which to defend oneself, that the other does not exist as anything but a projection of the self, is the same as recognizing that the immunitary system has no temporal or spatial limits. The immunitary system is always and everywhere. It coincides with our identity. We are identified with ourselves, definitively drawn away from being altered by the community.

And so? If this is our present condition, where do we turn? Is thinking community still viable? Is it possible to unite community and democracy again but in a different way? Can we imagine a nonimmunizing democracy that is likewise not immunized, or has the process of generalized immunization annihilated, along with community itself, the very possibility for thinking it? I don't believe we can. I don't think that the order of the day is to cease thinking community. On the contrary, I believe that today more than ever we should reactivate such thought. What else do the bodies, faces, expressions of millions of starving and deported people and refugees whose nude and terrifying images appear on our television screens from every corner of the world tell us? What else do they speak of, if not the question of community and its absence but also its necessity? Is it not still community—the relationship, our *cum*, "we" as *cum*—that is recalled in every birth and even the most anonymous, quotidian, seemingly banal encounter?

As always, what requires the most reflection is the least evident; the thing that requires the most reflection becomes the most difficult to think. Indeed, today as never before, the thought of community is exposed to the double risk of oblivion and distortion, of repression and betrayal. Thinking community risks oblivion above all because the end, the collapse of communism—of communism as a whole and of all communisms—produced a vacuum of ideas, like a whirlpool in which the question of community seems to have gotten caught up, submerged in the disrepute and disgrace of regimes that exploded or imploded under the weight of their errors and horrors. We may superimpose upon this danger of oblivion and erasure another, which is perhaps even graver: the perversion of the idea of community into its opposite, into one that erects walls rather than breaking them down. This happens far from us, on the periphery of the world, but also near us, at the center of our world, whenever community is reduced and impoverished to defend new individualisms, or small homelands that are closed and walled off from their outside, opposed and hostile to everything that does not belong to them, that retreats from the obsessive constraints of identity and what is considered to be properly their own. In this case, the image of the fortress is superimposed upon that of the desert, as the horizon of community is reversed while it takes a new and even more overbearing immunitary turn. What are the new ethnic, religious and linguistic communities that emerge not only on the other side of the Adriatic, in Asia and in Africa, but also in downtown Los Angeles, if not the most exasperated autoimmunization from common existence? What are they, if not a most brazen way of appropriating for oneself what appears to be claimed by another, if not an attempt to abolish every outside from an inside that is entirely folded in on itself in endogenous reproduction?

The idea of *communitas*—and earlier still, the idea of *munus* from which it is derived—moves in a direction that is radically opposed to such a relentless push toward immunitary interiorization (or perhaps we should say "internment"). *Communitas* recalls instead an exteriorization of existence, or, even better, an interpretation of existence itself as exteriority, experience, ecstasy (insofar as these expressions share a common root), as the subject's escape from himself or herself or as his or her originary opening to otherness that constitutes the subject from the beginning in the form of a "being-with" [*essere con*] or a "with-being" [*con-essere*]. *Être-avec* and *Mitsein*. These are the very perspectives advanced in the twentieth century by the two greatest philosophers of community, Martin Heidegger and Georges Bataille. Now I think we must resist the temptation to consider them only as philosophers—that is, as too distant from us and too abstract to face the problems of today. If we read them without being distracted by the particular density of their vocabularies, it will not escape us that they are talking precisely about this problem: the community as the exteriority of what appears closed-off to its own interior, the irreducible (because empty, comprised entirely of otherness) nucleus of that immunitarian system that seems ever more to circumscribe our horizon of meaning.

If these two philosophers pose the same question about what lies "outside" of the subject, or the subject's being "outside," they diverge on approaches. The possibilities for what we can infer about the basic query with which we began—how do we think, but also, how do we live the "common" in an age of immunization?—are likewise divergent. Where do we look for the outside of what presents itself only from within? Bataille's itinerary is fractured. His approach proceeds along the rupture of the immunitary cord and singles out possible points of contagion among the subjects who cross it. Bataille identifies the wounds through which social circulation may resume via the transmission of reciprocal lacks.[14] In this case, a return to the *munus* requires an idea of losing what is proper, of expropriation and weakening of what is one's own, that contests the very presupposition of immunitary logic: the conservation and the defense of the "self" from what threatens it from outside. He moves on to contest a restricted economy, as Bataille defines the utilitarian paradigm of our democracies, in favor of an enlarged or general economy that is dominated no longer by the imperative of accumulation but by the principle of unproductive expenditure, and therefore also by the gift. What Bataille outlines is, in fact, a conception of energetic abundance that is radically opposed to the neo-Hobbesian anthropological theory of the organic lack of animal-man upheld by Plessner and Gehlen. Whereas, as we have seen, this theory sets in motion a whole series of protective mechanisms aimed at freeing the individual from his communal bonds, Bataille recognizes within the stitching of the instinct of self-preservation an equally strong oppositional tendency toward the dissolution of individual identity in a common donative act of weakening what is one's own.

If Bataille interrogates the anthropological dimension of such a tendency, Heidegger shifts his attention to its ontological root. His question is not so much about the *inter* of *esse* but instead about the *esse* of *inter*—that is, not the sociality of being but being of *cum* and as *cum*. What does this mean with regard to the question of democracy? What does it mean that being itself has the same form as *cum*? How can we translate this *ontology of community* into our language?[15] We might begin with the simple proposition that community is, or, better still, "is given," regardless of our will, or our capacity to realize it. Community is also, and perhaps above all, given just as it seems to vanish from our horizon—just as, as we have said, it seems to transform itself into a desert, or deform itself into a fortress. Even the negation of community is something that belongs to our being common. It is a mode, however defective or negative, of community—as are solitude, conflict, and anomie. Indeed, Heidegger says something more about it (only then to clamorously contradict himself at other moments in his life and works). Against every temptation to conceive of community in terms of the "authentic" or the "proper," as the self-appropriation of one's own essence conducted by man, or by entire peoples, community always has to do with an inauthentic or improper modality. What is the "common" if not the improper, that which does not belong to anyone but instead is general, anonymous, indeterminate; that is not determined by essence, race, or sex but instead is pure existence exposed to the absence of meaning, foundation, and destiny?

There remains still another way of rereading Heidegger's *mit*, in light of his ambivalent evaluation of technology as an extreme danger but also as a potential resource. Here I have in mind the phenomenon of globalization, of which technology constitutes the last and most striking configuration. Globalization does not limit itself to representing technology; it is technology itself, spread out in a planetary power that meets no resistance or difference that it doesn't make a part of itself or subsume within its own model. In this sense, globalization also expresses the definitive closure of the immunitary system onto itself. Indeed, it is immunization driven to the sole principle of the regulation of individual and collective life in a world made identical with itself—made "global" [*mondializzato*]. Yet this "mondialization" carries within another outcome that surpasses the very horizon of Heidegger and Bataille. It doesn't coincide only with the destruction of meaning but also with its removal from every general principle, every given, anticipated, or prescribed meaning. Globalization is the world's return to a pure state of phenomenality: to its being nothing other than the world.[16] That is, if this is *the* only world, the *whole* world, it means that it is *only* the world; it is without presuppositions, origins, or ends that transcend its simple existence. From this perspective, wherein the progressive erosion of the nation-state and the modernity that produced it is seen as a unique turning point, such a planetary democracy may be thought, heeding all of the precautions and difficulties that this may present. Perhaps better still, the problem of democracy may be carried to the only level capable of wresting it from the immunitary drift for which it seems destined: the level of a world community—of the only world, that is, that we have in common. We know that immunization works through the controlled incorporation of the communitarian "germ" that it wants to neutralize. What if we attempted to reverse the operation? What if we tried to rethink community beginning by completing the process of immunization? After all, a world without an outside—that is, a world completely immunized—is by definition without an inside. At its most successful, immunization may also be propelled to immunize itself from itself in order to reopen the breach, or the time, of community.

FREEDOM AND IMMUNITY

Before taking up how the theme of freedom relates to community, I would like to consider something even more fundamental that involves the entire political lexicon and the growing difficulty such a lexicon faces in signifying its own object—namely, the political.[1] A true barrier seems to have been erected between language and politics. It is as if politics has escaped from language, as if language no longer has any words with which to name politics. As early as the 1930s, Simone Weil wrote, "On inspection, almost all the words and phrases of our political vocabulary turn out to be hollow."[2] What do we make of this feeling of emptiness, this draining of political vocabulary, this progressive and apparently unstoppable aphasia? Naturally, we might recall the abrupt transformations that have upset the international scene over the past decade and rendered previous categorical frameworks obsolete. This is what happened between the 1920s and 1930s, within a geopolitical horizon that was admittedly quite different from ours. What was then being formulated, literally eviscerating the political lexicon prior to its crisis, now explodes or implodes with analogous and linguistically disorienting effects.

Nevertheless, I believe that something more lies behind and within this political aphasia: a much older dynamic that ultimately concerns all of modern political philosophy, and more precisely its constitutively metaphysical character (in a sense similar to the one Heidegger attributed to the expression when he attempted to deconstruct the Western philosophical tradition). Without broadening the discussion to evaluate Heidegger's attempt, which is certainly problematic and contradictory, we might say that the metaphysical element of modern political philosophy—that is, what threatens to enclose it in a circular trajectory without exit—lies primarily in the superimposition that it presupposes between the spheres of meaning and sense, its tendency to reduce the horizon of sense for the great words of the political tradition to their most immediate and obvious meaning. It is as if philosophy limited itself to a frontal, direct approach to the categories of politics, as if philosophy were incapable of interrogating them obliquely, of sneaking up from behind, of entering the recessed layers of their meaning, the space of their being unthought. Every political concept has an illuminated part that is immediately visible, but also a dark zone, a cone of shade from which, only through contrast, such light bursts forth. Indeed we might say that contemporary political philosophy, and above all that of an analytic derivation, dazzled by such a light completely loses sight of that shady zone that surrounds, or cuts, political concepts and constitutes their horizon of sense in a form that in no way coincides with their manifest meaning. This is the case because, while the manifest meaning of political concepts is always univocal, monolinear, and self-enclosed, their underlying sense is more complex, often contradictory, and capable of containing reciprocally opposing elements, antinomic characteristics, which is to say a genuine conflict for the conquest of a more weighty significance. If we think about it, all the great words of our political tradition—namely, democracy, power, sovereignty—carry within, at their origin, this very antinomic, aporetic nucleus, this internal battle that makes these words irreducible to the linearity of their superficial meaning.

I attempted to get at this disparity, this unevenness between manifest meaning and underlying sense in my critical analysis of the idea of community. What came out of it was a genuine overturning of the definition that political philosophy assigns the concept. Whereas both American neocommunitarianism and organicistic German sociology link the idea of community to that of belonging, identity and ownership—that is, the community as something that identifies someone with his/her own ethnic group, land, or language—the originary term *community* has a radically different sense. One need only open a dictionary to learn that *common* is the exact contrary of *one's own*; common is what is *not* one's own, or what is unable to be appropriated by someone. It is what belongs to all or at least to many, and it therefore refers not to the same but to the other. If we trace the etymology of the Latin term *communitas*, we have immediate confirmation of this: The term is derived from *munus*, which means "gift," or even "obligation," toward another.³ Rather than being identified by a common belonging, what does it mean that the members of the community are bound instead by the duty of a reciprocal gift, by a law that conducts them outside of themselves in order to address the other, to the point of nearly expropriating himself in favor of this other?

But if this is where things stand—that is, if the idea of community expresses a loss, removal, or expropriation—if it recalls not a fullness, but a void and an alteration, this means that the idea of community is felt as a risk, a threat to the individual identity of the subject precisely because it loosens, or breaks, the boundaries that ensure the stability and subsistence of individual identity. It is because community exposes each person to a contact with, and also to a contagion by, an other that is potentially dangerous. In the face of precisely such a threat, which has been mythically transcribed in all of the accounts that associate the origin of the human community with a founding offense, modernity activates a process of immunization, following the paradigmatic clash between *communitas* and *immunitas*. If the former binds individuals to something that pushes them beyond themselves, then the latter reconstructs their identity by protecting them from a risky contiguity with the other, relieving them of every obligation toward the other and enclosing them once again in the shell of their own subjectivity. Whereas *communitas* opens, exposes, and turns individuals inside out, freeing them to their exteriority, *immunitas* returns individuals to themselves, encloses them once again in their own skin. Immunitas brings the outside inside, eliminating whatever part of the individual that lies outside. What is immunization if not the preventive interiorization of the outside, its neutralizing appropriation?

What I am suggesting is that the concept of freedom is subjected to the same closure, to the same neutralizing operation endured by community. How? Before approaching this question, let us ask another, preliminary one: Why should we still speak of freedom? Why add yet another meditation on freedom to the countless histories and philosophies of it which circulate today? I'd promptly answer that what I'm about to propose aims to be not a history, or a philosophy, of freedom but instead is an attempt to liberate freedom from history in order to restore it to what Jean-Luc Nancy defined as its "experience," the experience of freedom and freedom as experience (with all of the danger that the term *experience* contains etymologically).⁴ Perhaps the most apt answer is that the very inflation of discourses on freedom that occurs today—it's one of the most recurring words not only in political language but also in the media—signals a fundamental difficulty in articulating the concept. That is, one gets the impression that the more we talk about freedom, the more we claim and demand it, the more we emblazon it across all of our flags, the more freedom (both past and future) escapes us. Freedom becomes either an entity that once was but has since disappeared, like a star that has burned out but continues to recall an ever weakening light, or conversely, like a promise of something that is best kept at a certain distance so as not to see it explode with destructive effects of anarchy and terror (as Hegel said about absolute freedom).

Whether we declare that freedom has already been realized in our liberal democracies or defer it by claiming it belongs to a far-off tomorrow, we remain within the same interpretive model. That is, we remain within a subjectivist metaphysical framework wherein the political scene is occupied by a preformed and predefined subject—the individual—who regards freedom as an object to defend or conquer, to possess or extend. In this way, freedom is understood as a quality, a faculty, or a good that a collective subject or many subjects must acquire insofar as is possible—or as an obstacle that resists, or, conversely, yields, to being overcome by a subjective will that lies outside and before it. The subject exists prior to the freedom that he or she acquires, or attempts to acquire, in the face of necessity. There is a wall, a barrier, a door that the subject must force open or plow through; once that happens, he or she is free, freed or on the verge of being liberated. Nevertheless freedom is nothing but the residue, crack, or pressure hatch that necessity exercises on us. Freedom is a pure negative that the subject must wrest from what blocks and binds him or her if they want to be a true subject, a subject of his or her own freedom; a freedom that is appropriated and even constituted as subjective property. Freedom thus is understood as that which makes the subject the proprietor of himself or herself; as essentially "proper" and no longer "common."

The outcome of this subjectivist foundation in both philosophical and historical terms is easy to ascertain. Once conditioned to the act that establishes the subject—what post-Cartesian philosophy called the "free will" or "indeterminacy of the will"—freedom has not only seen its own horizon of sense reduced to an ever more impoverished meaning but has repeatedly found itself exposed to the risk of being overturned into its own logical opposition: and that is, in order (Hobbes), in sovereignty (Rousseau), and in the state (Hegel). In each case, what occurs within nearly all modern political philosophy, with the slight exception of Spinoza and, of course, Kant, is a logical passage that, beginning with an entirely subjective conception of freedom, transforms it into its opposite: an objective determination that is dialectically assumed by the would-be free subject. Otherwise, the subject endures it as the exterior price that the subject is obligated to pay for interior autonomy. Such is the position of Luther, according to whom even one who is outwardly in chains may be free in the most intimate, innermost recesses of his conscience. Likewise, all modern political philosophy ends up invariably restoring freedom to the realm of necessity, shifting seamlessly from a freedom that necessarily liberates to an unbridled necessity. Here we find ourselves on that slope, in that drift at the end of which Adorno may say that unfreedom "and freedom are so entangled that unfreedom is not just an impediment to freedom but a premise of its concept."[5]

How do we account for such an overturning of perspective? What motivates and produces it? Whence is this lexical contraction that reduces freedom to its bare opposite born? Probably from a fear of the power of the rupture, and even destruction, that the idea of freedom contains within itself; from the awareness, as Herman Broch once wrote, that freedom "is the volcano and lightning bolt of the human soul; this is why the keeper of the flame cannot help but burn himself on it repeatedly."[6] This would explain the need to construct a protective semantic barrier that ultimately enchains the experience of freedom in an ideal image that is destined to enclose its surplus sense within the confines of a meaning that is often presupposed—the need, we might say, to immure freedom, to suffocate its most acute and vibrant voice.

Here we may recall the category of immunization, which we introduced earlier in opposition to community. To fully grasp this shift, we'll need once again to return toward the originary sense implicit in the term "freedom." Well, surprising as it may be, what we may conclude is that at the origin of the idea of freedom lies something that links freedom to the very semantics of community. As Benveniste and others have demonstrated, both the Indo-European root *leuth,* or *leudh* (from which the Greek *eleutheria* and the Latin *libertas* derive), and the Sanskrit root *frya* (the source of the English *freedom* and the German *Freiheit*) recall something that has to do with a common growth. This is confirmed by the double semantic chain that descends from these roots: that of love (*lieben, life, love,* but perhaps also *libet* and *libido*) and that of affect and friendship (*friend*, *Freund*). Both roots unequivocally attest to the originally communitarian connotation of freedom. Freedom is a connective, aggregating, unifying power [*potenza*], even though, more than in the modern sense of "participation" it bears the sense of belonging to a common root that grows and develops according to its own internal law.[7] Therefore, freedom *in* and *as* a relationship: exactly the opposite of the autonomy and self-sufficiency of the individual to which for some time we have likened it. The originary sense of the idea of freedom is, therefore, anything but negative. It has nothing to do with the absence of an impediment, with the removal of a constraint, or with that which is exempt from oppression. Freedom carries a powerfully affirmative sense that is altogether political, biological, and physical, and which recalls an expansion, blossoming, or common growth, or a growth that brings together.

Now it is this extraordinary horizontal extension of the idea of freedom-relation (which is in some way present even in its Platonic and Aristotelian formulations) that will be progressively elided along with its affirmative declension: What was an immanent principle of development according to the intrinsic law of its own nature tends irresistibly to configure itself as the external perimeter that delimits what may be done from what should *not* be done. The juridicization of the Roman *libertas* already constitutes a primary contraction of the universality of the concept within an orbit that ultimately coincides with the borders of the *urbs* and its imperial dominions. Nevertheless the true immunitary turn takes place during the Middle Ages, when freedom—that is, every freedom—takes on the character of a "particular right": an ensemble of "privileges," "exemptions," or "immunity" (*iura et immunitates*; *Freiheiten* in German; *franchises* in French) that exempt certain collective subjects (classes, corporations, cities, convents) from an obligation that is common to all others and grant them a special juridical condition (like that of the *libertas ecclesiae*) within the hierarchical order. It is here that the passage from an open and affirmative notion of freedom to one that is restricted and negative, as well as immunized and immunizing, is carried out.

When, beginning with Hobbes and the model of natural law, modern political philosophy attempts to restore universality to the concept of freedom, it can only do so within an individualistic framework that has now been extended and multiplied by the number of individuals who are made equal by their reciprocal separation. Freedom is what separates the self from the other by restoring it to the self; it's what heals and rescues the self from every common alteration. From then on, with all of the possible variations—that is, from the absolutist—to the republican or the liberal type, freedom will always be conceived of as a right, good, or faculty of the individual who holds it, either through the protection of sovereign law (Hobbes) or, conversely, by protecting the individual from it (Locke). In both cases, this protection, first of life and then of individual property, assumes a starkly oppositional quality to the political dimension as such. As Arendt observes, beginning in the seventeenth and eighteenth centuries, freedom is tightly bound to security: We are free only insofar as and if we are secure—if freedom is "ensured" by its defensive and self-identifying connotation.[8] In this way, the "metaphysical" loop of freedom and necessity finally closes, despite and through the superficial opposition between a Republican paradigm (Montesquieu) and a liberal one (Constant), both of which are inscribed within and express in different ways the general immunization of freedom. Freedom's ultimate identification with property, not only by liberals but also, paradoxically, by the socialism of "free proprietors," merely constitutes the last passage of such an anticommunitarian drift: Free is he or she who is proprietor of what belongs to him or her. Freedom is nothing but the effect, or the consequence, of property; a figure of what is "proper," the opposite of what is "common." The tired contemporary opposition between *liberals* and *communitarians* [in English] only confirms such an immunitary outcome within a singular subjectivistic and individualistic lexicon, applied by some to individuals and by others to communities. Not to speak of the improbable theorizations of "liberal communities" that, in search of theoretical mediation and practical compromises among two concepts that are now separated by their immunitary conversion, reveal themselves as incapable of thinking both freedom and community, and moreover their originary, constitutive relationship. Wrested from the affirmative intensity of its ancient "common" root, freedom must now adapt to a solely negative declension: as non-dominion, non-constriction, and non-community. It's only represented with regard to the obstacles placed in the way of its impossible deployment; freedom risks speechlessness as the obstacles fall away (when in reality freedom merely absorbs these obstacles until they empty it of all effectiveness). Thus, we might say, we have lived in the "twilight of freedom"—as the great Russian poet Osip Mandel'shtam expressed—in which "We have roped swallows together in legions / Now we can't see the sun."[9] We have entered the "great year of twilight," in which freedom is chained to its own opposite, emptied of sense, and deprived of every factuality.

But freedom is either a fact or it is not. Either freedom grasps our experience such that freedom subsumes experience, or freedom remains blocked in the self-dissolving circle of idea, essence, or concept.[10] Therefore, freedom must be understood not as something that one has but as something that one is: what frees existence to the possibility to exist as such. A "decision of existence" that cannot become an object of theory, nor, precisely, of thought, but only a practice of experience. Pushing freedom to the limits of its philosophical meaning, Hegel wrote that freedom is the highest form of nothing per se; a negativity that is so intense that it is overturned, becoming an absolute affirmation. By this, he meant that freedom is nothing given, acquired, or permanent, that it is not a substance, a good, or a right to demand or defend. Freedom may not even coincide with itself: There is no freedom, only liberation, just as one cannot be but can only *become* free. That freedom is nothing, that it is founded upon nothing, that nothing lies behind it (as Schelling and Heidegger will variously say) means that freedom is pure beginning [*inizio*].[11] It is one with the commencement and birth of what comes into the world. According to Hannah Arendt, "Because he *is* a beginning, man can begin; to be human and to be free are one and the same."[12] It is in this originary and radical meaning that men are free.

Why and in what sense are men free? What is the most intense and extreme sense of freedom? What is a freedom that is ultimately free to be such? At the conclusion of every philosophy of freedom another way of understanding it seems to take shape, one about which we know neither the meaning nor the name. The great series of reflections that runs from Kant to Heidegger, via Schelling, certainly comes close. As does, perhaps even more, an inclination, or a decision for freedom that profoundly affects the most important poetry of the past two centuries, from Baudelaire to Mandelstam, from Hölderlin to Celan. Just as something about that coming freedom, as an event and an advent, flashes here and there within the words of Sartre, Adorno, Anders and Bataille, Foucault and Deleuze. But such instances of freedom as an event and an advent do not suffice. They do not suffice in reversing a current that seems to drag freedom toward a destined outcome, toward its very negation. It's not enough to free freedom, as Rimbaud once hoped in vain when, just before cutting all ties with the past, he wrote to Izambard: "I stubbornly continue to love freedom."[13] The only way of rescuing freedom from such a destiny, the only way to revitalize and restore freedom's affirmative power, is perhaps to guide it back to its primary sense by reconstructing the semantic node that originally bound it to community, to the aggregating power of a common root. Here, I intend community not as a locus of identity, belonging, or appropriation but, on the contrary, as a locus of plurality, difference, and alterity. It is an option that is both philosophical and political, and one in which I believe the very task of contemporary political philosophy lies: liberating freedom from liberalism and community from communitarianism. That is, we must deconstruct the first and most entrenched of those false antitheses that modern political philosophy has built in an attempt to fill in the void of thought that it has carved out around and within the great concepts of politics. If it is thought affirmatively, freedom can only be "common"—belonging to each and all because it's not proper to anyone. Which is to say, it's an expression of the very *munus* that is originally shared by the members of the *communitas*: "The bestower of freedom is only free in others" (*Le donneur de liberté n'est libre que dans les autres*).[14] And again: "At all the meals taken in common, we invite freedom to have a seat. Its place remains empty but it stays set."[15] What Char means is that freedom only exists in the place of the in-common, even if, and perhaps above all because, that place is empty. To conclude: What does it mean that freedom occupies the empty place of community? What does it mean that the emptiness of community, and as community, is the very place of freedom? Community and freedom share the same *munus*. One is the gift of the other and through the other. Yet what is this *munus*, this gift and this law, that liberates the community just as it restores to freedom a common dimension? How do the terms *community* and *freedom*, however different, intersect with one another without becoming identical?

We might say that freedom is the singular dimension of community. It is community itself in its infinitely singular space—and only for this reason is it also plural. It is neither community in the singular, nor even a singular community but a community that sweeps across infinite singularities that *are* plurality. If it's true that community is neither subject nor common substance but a way of being in common of singularities that are irreducible to one another, then freedom coincides with that irreducibility. It is the gap, limit, or threshold that sculpts community into a shape that is "every time," or "from time to time," or "one at a time." Freedom confronts community with its own outside, or projects that outside within as it is, without neutralizing community preventively. We might say that freedom is the internal exteriority of community: the part of community that resists immunization, that is not identical to itself, and that remains open to difference. It is the beginning, pulsing, or crack that suddenly opens in community—a community that opens itself to the singularity of every existence. This is the experience of freedom.

IMMUNIZATION AND VIOLENCE

In an essay dedicated to Kant as an interpreter of the Enlightenment, Michel Foucault identifies the task of contemporary philosophy in a certain kind of attitude. It has to do with our strained relationship to the present that he calls the "ontology of actuality." What does he mean? What does it mean to place philosophy at the point, or on the line, in which actuality reveals itself in all the richness of its historicity? What exactly does *ontology of actuality* mean? First of all, the expression implies a shift of the gaze inward, toward ourselves. Situating ourselves ontologically within the present means considering modernity no longer as an era among others but as the tendency or the will to see our own present as a task. In such a call there is something, call it a tension, impulse, or what Foucault calls an *ēthos*, that moves beyond the Hegelian definition of philosophy as our own time understood through thought, because situating ourselves ontologically within the present makes thought the lever that wrests the present from the linear continuity of time, suspending thought from making a decision on what we are and what we may be. For Kant, an allegiance to the Enlightenment meant not only being loyal to certain ideas or accepting the autonomy of man; above all, Enlightenment meant setting in motion a never-ending critique of our own historicity. Rather than refuting or negating the present or abandoning it in favor of an unrealizable utopia, enlightenment meant inverting the notion of the possible that the present contains, making the present the basis for a different reading of reality.

This is the task of philosophy as an ontology of actuality. In analytical terms, it means identifying the difference between the essential and the contingent—that is, between the superficial effects and the deep-rooted dynamics that propel events, transform lives, and mark existence. Philosophy's task is to seize the moment, the critical threshold in which daily news takes on the richness of history. The task of philosophy as an ontology of actuality raises fundamental questions about the meaning of what we call "today." What do we really mean by *today*? What are the essential characteristics of today, its realities, contradictions, and potentialities? Still this question doesn't exhaust the role of an ontology of actuality. It is merely the condition for another question, which now takes the form of a choice or a decision. What does thought necessarily assume as a given about the present and what else—that is, what latent possibilities—might it reawaken and liberate? What part of the present should we side with, risk something for, or bet on? Because thought should not be limited to describing what it is, the lines of force that traverse our moment; thought should recognize actuality as the epicenter of a comparison and a confrontation between two different and opposing perspectives within which thought itself is situated. Thought is always to be found on the mobile border between outside and inside, between process and event, between the real and the possible. This border, limit, or field is the very locus of philosophy: its horizon of meaning and its contemporary destiny.

This is the question, or the choice, that has informed my recent work. It's an attempt to identify the key terms, the paradigms around which the coordinates of a given historical moment are structured—in ways that are not always visible to the naked eye. This was, at least, the question with which I began and which I now want to answer. What are the conflicts, traumas, or nightmares, but also the demands or hopes, that most characterize the present moment? I think I've traced this key term, this general paradigm, in the category of immunity or immunization. What do I mean? We all know that, in biomedical language, immunity names a form of exemption from, or protection against an infectious disease; in the juridical lexicon immunity represents a sort of safeguard that makes someone beyond the common law. In both cases, therefore, immunization refers to a particular situation that saves someone from the risks to which the entire community is exposed. Here we can see the fundamental opposition between community and immunity that informs my recent reflections. Without discussing the merits of complex etymological questions, let's simply say that immunity (or, in Latin, *immunitas*) is the opposite of *communitas*. Both words derive from the term *munus*, which means "gift," "duty," "obligation," but *communitas* is affirmative while *immunitas* is negative. Thus, if the members of the community are characterized by an obligation to give a gift, by this law to care for the other, immunity implies the exemption or exception from such a condition. He or she who is shielded from the obligation and the dangers that affect all others is immune. Immune is he or she who breaks the circuit of social circulation by placing himself or herself outside it.

I want to propose two fundamental theses. The first is that this immunitary *dispositif*, which is to say, this need for exemption and protection that originally belonged to the medical and juridical fields, has spread to all sectors and languages of our lives, to the point that the immunitary *dispositif* has become the coagulating point, both real and symbolic, of contemporary existence. Certainly every society has expressed a need to be protected. Every collectivity has posed a fundamental question about how to preserve life. My impression, however, is that only today, at the end of the modern period, has such a need become the linchpin around which both the real and imaginary practices of an entire civilization have been constructed. To get a rough idea of what I mean, consider simply the role that immunology—that is, the science charged with the study and the reinforcement of immune systems—has shouldered not only medically but also socially, juridically, and ethically. Think what the discovery of the immunodeficiency syndrome AIDS has meant for the normalization—that is, the subjection to precise norms that are not only health and hygiene related—of individual and collective experience. Or both the prophylactic and sociocultural barriers that the nightmare of the disease has created in all human relationships. Moving from the realm of infectious diseases to the social realm of immigration confirms this: The fact that the growing flows of immigrants are thought (entirely erroneously) to be one of the worst dangers for our societies also suggests how central the immunitary question is becoming. Everywhere we look, new walls, new blockades, and new dividing lines are erected against something that threatens, or at least seems to, our biological, social, and environmental identity. It is as if that fear of being even accidentally grazed has been made worse, that fear that Elias Canetti located at the origin of our modernity in a perverse short circuit between touch [*tatto*], contact [*contatto*], and contagion [*contagio*]. The risk of contamination immediately liquidates contact, relationality, and being in common.

We might say the same about information technology: Here again, the greatest problem, the real nightmare of all systems operators, are so-called computer viruses that affect not only handheld devices but large information systems that regulate financial, political, and military relationships on a global scale. By now all Western governments allocate enormous sums to keep antiviral programs up to date so that they can immunize their computer networks from infiltration by pathogenic agents and possible terrorist attacks. The fact that today, at the heart of the most important national and international affairs, a juridical battle over the immunity of certain political personages is taking place (as there was for Pinochet and Milosevic, and many others) further proves my point. What is feared, more than individual cases, is a weakening of the sovereign power of single states, a breaking up of the juridical boundaries of the national order that favors some yet-to-be-constructed form of international justice. The point is that wherever you look, what is happening in the world today, from the individual body to the social one, from the technological body to the political one, you will find the question of immunity placed at their intersection. What is important is inhibiting, preventing, and fighting the spread of contagion wherever it presents itself, using whatever means necessary.

As I've said, this preoccupation with self-protection isn't only a condition of the present moment. Yet the threshold of awareness with regard to risk has differed over time. And still today such an awareness is at its greatest, due to a series of aggravating factors related to what we call globalization: The more human beings, as well as ideas, languages, and technologies, communicate and are bound up with one another, the more necessary preventative immunization as a counterweight becomes. New withdrawals into localized interests might be explained as a sort of immunitary rejection of that global contamination that is globalization. The more the "self" tends to make itself "global," the more the self must struggle to include inside what is outside; the more the self tries to introject every form of negativity, the more negativity is reproduced. It was precisely the breaking down of the great real and symbolic Berlin Wall that caused so many small walls to go up and that transformed and perverted the very idea of community into a besieged fortress. What matters most is limiting an excess of circulation and therefore of potential contamination. Thus, the virus has become the widespread metaphor for all of our nightmares. In reality, there was a moment in our societies when fear, at least the biological kind, had subsided. I have in mind the 1950s and 1960s, when the optimistic idea that antibiotics could do away with some millenary diseases held sway. And so it was, until AIDS appeared, at which point the psychological dam gave way. Viruses both symbolic and real reemerged and seemed invincible; real demons capable of working their way inside us and dragging us into their void of no-sense. At that point the demand for immunity grew massively until it became our fundamental commitment, the very form that we gave our lives.

My second thesis is here: The idea of immunity, which is needed for protecting our life, if carried past a certain threshold, winds up negating life. That is, immunity encages life such that not only is our freedom but also the very meaning of our individual and collective existence lost: that flow of meaning, that encounter with existence outside of itself that I define with the term *communitas*, which refers to the constitutively open character of existence. Heidegger would call it the *ex* of *existentia*. This is the terrible contradiction that we ought to focus on: What safeguards the individual and collective body is the same thing that slows down its development and that, beyond a certain point, winds up destroying it. To borrow the language of Walter Benjamin (who himself died because of a border closure) we might well say that immunization in high doses means sacrificing every form of qualified life, for reasons of simple survival: the reduction of life to its bare biological layer, of *bíos* to *zoé*. To remain such, life is forced to bend to an outside power [*potenza*] that penetrates and crushes it. Life is forced to incorporate that nothing that it wishes to avoid, as life is fixed within its significative void.

On the other hand, this contradiction, which is the antinomic connection between the protection and the negation of life, is implicit in the very procedure of medical immunization: We know that, in order to vaccinate a patient against a disease, you have to introduce a controlled and tolerable portion of it into the organism. It follows that medicine here is made of the same poison from which it has to protect us; it's almost as if to save someone's life they need to taste death. Moreover, the term *phármakon* originally has the meanings of both "cure" and "poison," which is to say poison as a cure, a cure by poisoning. It's as if modern immunitary procedures had carried this contradiction of cure and poison to its zenith: The cure is given in the form of a lethal poison. If we bring this immunological practice to bear on the social body, we see the same antinomy, the same counterfactual paradox: Raising society's threshold of attention with regard to risk, as has been the case for some time now, means blocking the growth of the social body, or even causing it to regress to its primitive state. It would seem that, instead of adjusting the level of protection to the actual presence of risk, we were adjusting instead the perception of risk to the growing demand for protection. That is, risk is artificially created in order to control it, as insurance companies do all the time. All of this is part of modern experience. Yet it's my impression that we're moving toward a point, a limit at which this reciprocally recharging mechanism of insurance and risk, of protection and negation of life, risks spiraling out of control. To have a nonmetaphorical idea of what I mean, consider what happens in autoimmune diseases when the immune system becomes so strong that it turns against the very mechanism that should be defended and winds up destroying it. Certainly, we need immune systems. No individual or social body could do with out them, but when they grow out of proportion they end up forcing the entire organism to explode or implode.

In light of the tragic events of September 11, 2001, the destruction of immune systems is really what threatens us. I believe that the current war is closely tied to the immunitary paradigm;[1] the war is the form that its intensification and its madness takes. The war is the tragic epilogue of what we might call an "immunitary crisis," in the same way that René Girard uses the expression *sacrificial crisis* to describe the moment when the logic of sacrifice exceeds the boundaries of the single victim and drags society as a whole into violence. Blood then spurts from everywhere, and human beings literally fall to pieces. In other words, the present conflict appears to burst forth from the dual pressure of two immunitary obsessions that are both opposed and specular: an Islamic extremism that is determined to protect to the death what it considers to be its own religious, ethnic, and cultural purity from contamination by Western secularization, and a West that is bent on excluding the rest of the planet from sharing in its own excess goods. As soon as these two oppositions were bound together, the entire world was convulsed by what resembled the most devastating autoimmune disease: A surplus of defense with regard to elements outside the organism had turned against the organism, with potentially lethal effects. What exploded along with the Twin Towers was the dual immunitary system that until then had kept the world intact.

Let's remember that this tragic event took place entirely within the mono-theistic triangle of Christianity, Judaism, and Islam, the real and symbolic epicenter of which is Jerusalem. Everything happened, everything was bound to and then was let loose, within the vicious cycle of monotheism, and not in the Buddhist or Hindu world. Why? I would say that both Islamic and Christian civilizations, through Judaism, faced off not in terms of how they were different (as the theorists of the clash of civilizations would have it) but instead in terms of how they were similar and all joined in their constitutive categories to the logic of the One, which is to say to the syndrome of mono-theism. The fact that in the East this takes on the shape of the one and only God and in the West of our true god, which is to say money as an absolute value, doesn't make any difference. The fact is that both logics are subjected to the principle of Unity. Both mean to unify the world according to their own points of view. Before oil, land, and bombs, these are what I would call the metaphysical stakes of this war. Paradoxically, what is at stake here is the question of truth, a clash with no quarter between two partial truths that aim to present themselves as global truths. At stake is also a confrontation within the monotheistic model itself (or at least within a political or po-liticized monotheism), since religious monotheisms contain other kinds of spiritual treasures. On one side, we find the full truth of Islamic fundamen-talism, according to which truth coincides with itself, the one written in the Koran and poised to conquer the world. On the other side, we find the empty truth of Western nihilism and secularized Christianity, according to which the truth is that the truth doesn't exist; what counts instead are the principle of technological performance, the logic of profit, and total production. It's these two truths—one full, the other empty; one present to itself, the other drawn within its own absence, but both absolute, exclusive, and excluding—that meet each other within the same immunitary obsession to conquer the global world, or the global-ness of a world reflected back on itself until it ex-plodes. Political monotheism—the idea that one king and one kingdom must correspond to one God—expresses the very essence of immunization at its most violent: border closings that do not tolerate anything from the outside, that exclude the very idea of an outside, that do not admit any foreignness that might threaten the logic of the One-and-everything [l'Uno-tutto].

Without wanting to open a discussion about the political, social, and cul-tural responsibilities for such a state of affairs, I'd insist on this undeniable fact: Entrusted to an autoimmunitary regime that is obsessively concerned with its own identity, the world or all of human life isn't likely to survive. When increased to the point that at which it turns into its opposite, the negative protection of life will end up destroying, along with the enemy outside, its own body. The violence of interiorization, which is to say the abolition of an outside, of the negative, could turn into an absolute exteriorization, a complete negativity. So what can we do? How can we snap this deathly logic? How can we recognize, as the ontology of actuality requires, the point at which the overturning of the present can move toward other alternatives? None of us has a perfect answer ready at hand. Clearly we know what we can't do. We can't go back to the "Westphalia model," to the concert of fully sovereign and free states that dominated the international scene for nearly five centuries. Just as we can't construct an equilibrium between two blocks such as the one that dominated from the end of the Second World War to the last decade of the twentieth century. Yet a return to a constellation of places defined by ethnicity, soldered together through a close relationship between land, blood, and language, is likewise unimaginable. In my opinion, the path to follow is not along what appears to be the only dialectic between global and local, and to which almost all current political philosophies seem to refer, but is instead one that is in line with the construction of a new relationship between the singular and the global. This is, however, only thinkable outside, or after having broken, the monotheistic paradigm and its constitutively immunitary logic. Most fundamentally, the question that allows critical thinking *in* and *of* the present, is: What seeps out from the theological-political vocabulary in which we are still entrenched, as the monotheistic syndrome I've been discussing clearly illustrates? And here I'm not speaking about the Islamic world but of the West that is, in its very secularization, up to its knees in political theology, as Carl Schmitt wrote.

Leaving behind the theological-political lexicon that underpins all of our categories, beginning with sovereignty and running through that of the legal personality, certainly isn't easy. Nevertheless, we don't have a choice. We can't return to a world of internally autonomous pieces potentially hostile to their own outside. At the same time, proceeding with this globalization of a "self" that is incapable of stepping outside of itself and turn outward toward its own outside is impossible. It would mean holding on to the destructive and self-destructive logic of *immunitas*, when it is actually a question of thinking about its opposite: the open and plural form of *communitas*. The world, which is at this point inextricably united, should be not only thought but "practiced" as an ensemble of differences, or a system of distinctions, in which distinction and difference are not points of resistance to or residues of the processes of globalization but their very form. Naturally, I know very well that transforming this philosophical formula into actual practice, into a political logic, isn't easy. And yet we have to find a way, a form, or a conceptual language that converts the immunitary declension that all political fundamentalisms have taken on into a singular and plural logic in which differences become precisely what holds the world together. I believe that the West, if we can use this category in a non-defensive or inoffensive way, has the strength, the economic and cultural resources, to undertake this radical operation of conversion, to use this last term in its most powerful sense. The West can do so despite its recurring temptation to make the world over into one model. Ever since Heraclitus, the idea that we may be joined together not by what we share but by distinction and diversity is part of the Western tradition, but it's an idea that was never achieved. Repression and oblivion mark much of the violent history of the West. The tragic paradox that we are living today lies in the fact that those who declared war on the West have reproduced and strengthened to the point of paroxysm the very same phobic obsession, the same conviction that no community or relationship among different peoples exists that is not an autoimmune, mortal encounter.

When the most destructive tendencies reflect one another and redouble into the same mad dash toward massacre, the only possibility that remains is to shatter the mirror in which the self is reflected without seeing anything but itself, or to break the spell. The great French linguist Émile Benveniste reminds us that the Latin pronoun *sé*, like its modern derivations, carries within it an ancient Indo-European root—from which the Latin *suus* and *soror* and the Greek *éthos* and *étes*, which mean "relative," or "ally," derive. Benveniste thus deduces that at the origins of this root lie two distinctive semantic lines. The first refers to the individual and private self, expressed by *ídios* (belonging to one's self). The second refers to a larger sphere in which many subjects interact with each other: hence the terms *hetaîros* and *sodalis*, both of which express a communitarian bond—something that is common to those who are characterized by it, as in the *munus* of *communitas*. From here we see the complex relationship between the reflexive *se* of "by himself" and the distinctive and disjunctive *se* of *sed*, which affirms that at the origin of what we call "oneself" is precisely an unbreakable nexus of unity and distinction, of identity and otherness. Without giving too much weight to etymology, perhaps in the depths of our linguistic tradition we might find the key to inverting, as Foucault said, the lines of the present in order to liberate, in the present-ness of its history, a different possibility that is just as available [*presente*], even if it has never truly been experienced.

BIOPOLITICS AND PHILOSOPHY

More than fear or hope, perhaps surprise is what recent international events have made us feel. Before they turn out to be positive, negative, or even tragic, international events are first and foremost unexpected. Moreover, they seem to contradict all reasonable calculation of probability. From the sudden and bloodless collapse of the Soviet system in 1989 to the terrorist attacks of September 11, 2001, and everything that followed, what we can say at a minimum is not only that we couldn't have imagined them before they occurred but that everything appeared to make their occurrence unlikely. Naturally, every collective event carries a certain degree of unpredictability, as history always shows. And yet, even when we are dealing with major discontinuities, such as revolutions or wars, one may always say that paving the way for these events, or at least allowing them, were various conditions that certainly made them possible, if not probable. We might say the same about the forty years that followed the end of the Second World War, when the world's bipolar order left no margin for the unforeseen to occur, to the point that what was taking place in each of the two blocks appeared to be the almost automatic result of a game all of whose moves were well-known and predictable.

All of this—that is, this political order that seemed bound to govern international relations for many years to come—suddenly burst: first in the form of implosion (in the case of the Soviet system) and then in an explosion (in the case of terrorism). Why? How can we explain the sudden change, and where exactly does it come from? The most frequent response has to do with the end of the Cold War and the advent of globalization that followed. Put this way, we risk mistaking cause for effect, offering as an explanation something that instead requires explanation. Even the recent hypothesis of the so-called clash of civilizations names an emergency, or at least the presence of risk in the most dramatized terms, yet it does not allow an adequate interpretation. Why in the world would civilizations (if we want to use such a rigid term), after having lived together peacefully for more than half a millennium, today threaten to clash with catastrophic results? Why is international terrorism spreading so perniciously? And why are Western democracies seemingly incapable of meeting it without resorting to instruments and strategies that over the long term undermine these democracies' founding values? The typical answer, namely the growing crisis of democratic institutions and the difficulty of marrying individual and collective rights, freedom and security, also remains within an interpretive circle that instead should be opened. The impression is that we're continuing to move within a semantics that's no longer capable of interpreting contemporary reality, or that in any case we remain on the surface or at the margins of a much deeper movement. The truth is that as long as we stand pat with this excessive classical language of rights, democracy, and freedom, we won't be able to recognize the newness of the situation, whose radical novelty puts the preceding period in a different light. What doesn't work in the answers provided, more than the individual conceptual references, is the overall framework within which references are situated. Within such a framework, how can we understand the choice of suicide for kamikaze terrorists, or even the antinomy of so-called humanitarian wars that end up devastating the very populations that they aim to save? How do we reconcile the idea of preventive war with the option of peace shared by all democratic states, or even with the secular principle of not interfering in the affairs of other sovereign states? The entire structure of modern political categories is of no help, as it hinges upon a bipolarity between individual rights and state sovereignty, which makes a resolution impossible. It's not merely a question of whether the lexicon is appropriate or not, or whether the perspective works or doesn't but rather has to do with the real effect of concealing: It's as if that lexicon wound up hiding something else behind its semantic curtain, another scene or logic that has been emerging, but has only recently come to light so explosively. What is this other scene, this logic or object that modern political philosophy cannot express and which it tends to hide?

My feeling is that we must touch on that ensemble of events which, at least since the time of Michel Foucault's work (though actually emerging a decade or so before him), was called biopolitics. Without pausing here to write a genealogy of the concept,[1] and not wanting to reflect on the various meanings that biopolitics acquired over time (and even within Foucault's *oeuvre* itself), we can say that, in its most general formulation, biopolitics refers to the increasingly intense and direct involvement established between political dynamics and human life (understood in its strictly biological sense), beginning with a phase that we can call second modernity. Of course we know that politics has always had something to do with life—that life, even in the biological sense, has always constituted the material frame within which politics is necessarily inscribed. How can we fail to place the agrarian politics of the ancient empires, or the politics of hygiene and sanitation developed in Rome, within the category of the politics of life? And doesn't the ancient regime's corporeal domination of slaves, or more still, the power of life or death exercised on prisoners of war imply a direct and immediate relationship between power and *bíos*? Furthermore, Plato, in particular in the *Republic*, the *Statesman* and the *Laws*, advises eugenic practices that go as far as to advocate the infanticide of babies suffering from weak constitutions. Yet, none of this is enough to locate these events and texts within a properly biopolitical orbit. The reason? Because, in the ancient and medieval periods, preserving life as such was never the primary objective of political action, as it was to become in the modern era. As Hannah Arendt reminded us, a preoccupation with the maintenance and reproduction of life for some time actually was part of a sphere that was neither political nor public but economic and private until real political action took on meaning and importance precisely in contrast to it.

Perhaps it's with Hobbes, and in the era of the religious wars, that the question of life embeds itself in the very heart of political theory and practice. The Leviathan State is instituted in defense of life, and subjects hand over the powers they naturally possess in exchange for protection by the state in the name of life. All of Hobbes's political categories (not to mention those of the authoritarian or liberal writers who succeed him)—namely sovereignty, representation, the individual—are in reality simply linguistic and conceptual modalities for naming or translating the biopolitical question of safeguarding human life from the dangers of violent extinction that threaten it into politicophilosophical terms. Therefore, we might even go so far as to say that it wasn't that modernity posed the question of the self-preservation of life but rather that life brings into being, or "invents," modernity as the complex of categories capable of answering the question of the preservation of life. What we call modernity, in other words, taken as a whole, might be nothing more than the language that allowed us to give the most effective answers to a series of requests for self-protection that sprang forth from the very foundations of life.[2] Here such a demand for salvific narratives such as, for example, the social contract, would have been born and would have become increasingly pressing as the defenses that until then had constituted the symbolic shell protecting human experience (beginning with the theological perspective of transcendence) began to grow weaker. Once these natural defenses rooted in common sense—this sort of primitive immunitary wrapping—had failed, an additional, now artificial, *dispositif* was needed to protect human life from risks that had become increasingly unbearable, such as those caused by civil wars or foreign invasions. Because he was projected toward the outside in a way that had never before been experienced, modern man required a series of immunitary apparatuses to protect a life made identical to itself from the secularization of religious references. Here, traditional political categories, such as order, but also freedom, take on meaning that forces them ever more toward the shelter of security measures. Freedom, for example, ceases to be understood as participation in the political management of the *pólis* and is now recast in terms of personal security along a fault line that follows us to this very moment: Free is he who is able to move without fearing for his life and property.

This doesn't mean, however, that we're still working today within the field of inquiry that Hobbes gave birth to, nor does it mean that his categories can be employed in the current situation; if it were otherwise, we wouldn't find ourselves facing a need to propose a new political language. Actually, between the era that we can generically call modern and our own, we find a sharp discontinuity that we can locate in the first decades of the twentieth century, when true biopolitical reflection gains a foothold. What is this difference? In the first modernity, the relationship between politics and the preservation of life (as Hobbes understood it) was still mediated, filtered through a paradigm of order that is expressed within the previously mentioned concepts of sovereignty, representation, and individual rights. In the second phase (which, in different and inconsistent ways, we still are a part of), that mediation has progressively disappeared, and in its place we have a greater overlapping of politics and *bíos*. Signaling this shift is the greater weight that the politics of public health, demography, and urban life have within the logic of the government beginning as early as the end of the eighteenth century. This is, however, merely the first step toward a biopoliticization of all societal relationships. Foucault analyzed various key points along this process of the governmentalization of life—that is, from so-called pastoral power, tied to the Catholic practice of confession, to *raison d'état* and the knowledge practices of the "police," which at one time included all the practices that aimed at material well-being.[3] From that moment on, the maintenance, development, and expansion of life becomes of strategic political relevance. Life is decisively put into play in political conflicts. At the same time, politics itself begins to be shaped according to biological and especially medical models.

We all know that this comingling of political and biomedical languages enjoys a long history. Consider, for example, the millennium-long duration of the "political body," or just the political terms that come to us from biological ones, like *nation* or *constitution*. But the double and crisscrossing politicization of life and the biologization of politics that unfolds at the opening of the twentieth century means something else as well, not only because life increasingly moves to the heart of the political game but because, under certain conditions, this biopolitical vector is turned into its thanatopolitical opposite, thereby linking the battle for life to a practice of death. This is the question that Foucault baldly poses when he asks a question that continues to interpellate us today: How does a politics of life continually threaten to become a practice of death?[4] Such a result was already implicit in what I called the immunitary paradigm of modern politics, by which I meant the growing tendency to protect life from the risks that inhere in the relationship among men and women even at the cost of ending communitarian bonds (which is what Hobbes describes, for example).[5] In the same way that someone is protected beforehand from contagion, a portion of the disease is injected into the very body that one intends to protect; in social immunization, life is guarded in a form that negates what is life's most intense shared meaning. Yet a truly fatal leap occurs when this immunitary turn in biopolitics intersects with the trajectory of nationalism, and then racism. Then, the question of conserving life shifts from the individual (typical of the modern period) to that of the nation-state as well as the population, which is seen as an ethnically defined body placed in opposition to other states and other populations. As soon as the life of a racially characterized people is viewed as the supreme value to keep in line with its originary constitution (or even to expand beyond those borders), obviously the lives of other peoples and other races tend to be felt as an obstacle and are therefore to be sacrificed to the life of that racially defined people. *Bíos* is thus artificially cut by a series of thresholds in zones of varying value that subordinate part of it to the violent and destructive domination of the other.

The one philosopher who understood this most radically, in part because he made it his own point of view, and in part because he criticized its nihilistic results, is Nietzsche. When he talks about the will to power as the very foundation of life, or when he places the very body of individuals at the center of interhuman dynamics and not conscience, he makes life the sole subject and object of politics. The fact that life is the will to power for Nietzsche means not that life wants power or that power determines life from the outside but that life knows no other way of being than a continual strengthening [*potenziamento*]. What condemns modern institutions—that is, the state, Parliament, the political parties—to inefficiency is their incapacity to locate themselves at this level of the discourse. Nietzsche, however, doesn't stop there. The extraordinary importance as well as the risk of his perspective on biopolitics lies not only in his having placed biological life, the body, at the center of political dynamics but also in the absolute lucidity with which he foresees that the definition of human life—the decision about what constitutes a true human life—will become the most crucial object of conflict in the centuries to come. When he asks in a well-known passage, "why shouldn't we be able to accomplish with human beings what the Chinese have learned to do with trees—that it carries roses on one side and pears on the other?" we have before us an extremely delicate transition from a politics of the administration of biological life to one able to glimpse the possibility of life's artificial transformation.[6] Human life here becomes the terrain of decisions that have to do with not only its external thresholds—that is, what distinguishes it from animal or vegetal life, for example—but also inner thresholds. This means that politics will be allowed to, will even be asked to, decide what is a biologically better life, and also how to strengthen it through the use, the exploitation, or, when necessary, the death of a "worse" life.

Twentieth-century totalitarianism, but especially that of the Nazis, signals the apex of this thanatopolitical drift. The life of the German people becomes the biopolitical idol for which every other people who were seen as contaminating and weakening that life from within will be sacrificed (in particular this meant the Jewish people). Never more than here did the immunitary *dispositif* register such an absolute convergence between the protection and the negation of life. The supreme strengthening of the life of a race that pretends to be pure is paid for with the large-scale production of death: first that of others, and, finally, in the moment of defeat, of their own, as is demonstrated by the order of self destruction signed by a Hitler under siege in his Berlin bunker. As in so-called autoimmune diseases, here too the immune system is strengthened to the point of fighting the very body that it should be saving, but it is now causing that body's decomposition. It makes little sense to obscure the absolute specificity of what happened in Germany in the 1930s and 1940s. The category of totalitarianism, however valuable it was for calling attention to certain connections between antidemocratic systems of the time, risks erasing, or at a minimum shading over, the irreducible character of Nazism not only with respect to modern political categories (of which Nazism signals their collapse) but also with regard to Stalinist communism.

While Stalinist communism may still be seen as an explosive extreme of the philosophy of modern history, Nazism lies entirely outside not only modernity but the philosophical tradition of modernity. Yet it does have its own philosophy, but it is completely translated into biological terms.[7] Nazism was not, as communism wished to be, the fulfillment of philosophy. Rather Nazism was the realization of biology. If the transcendental—that is, the constitutive category from which all others derive—of communism is history, for Nazism that category is life, understood from the point of view of a comparative biology that distinguishes between human races and animal ones. This explains the absolutely unprecedented role that both anthropologists, working side by side with zoologists, and doctors played in Nazism. For the former, the politically central role of anthrozoology resulted from the importance that Nazis awarded the category of *humanitas* (in fact, a celebrated handbook of racial politics had this very name),[8] which was continually re-elaborated through the definition of biological thresholds between worthy and unworthy lives, as the infamous book on "life unworthy of life" suggests.[9] For the latter, the direct participation of doctors in all the phases of the genocide, namely from the selection of the camp slopes to the final cremation of prisoners, is well known and widely documented. As we can deduce from their declarations about the various activities in which they were involved, medical doctors understood their death work to be the very mission of the doctor: curing the German body from a grave illness by eliminating the infected part and the invasive germs once and for all. To their eyes, this work was a great disinfestation, necessary in a world besieged by biological degeneration, in which the Jewish race constituted the most lethal element.

From this perspective, Nazism establishes an element of rupture and also a pivot within biopolitics. Nazism carried that element to its point of greatest antinomy, summed up in the principle that life is protected and developed only by progressively enlarging the sphere of death. Nazism also radically alters the logic of sovereignty. Whereas, at least in its classical formulation, only the sovereign maintains the right to life and death of his subjects, all citizens of the Reich are endowed with this right. If it's a question of the racial defense of the German people, all can legitimately, and indeed are even required to, bring about the death of all others and ultimately, if the situation requires it (as in the moment of final defeat), even their own deaths. Here the defense of life and the production of death truly meet at a point of absolute indistinction. The sickness that the Nazis wanted to eliminate was the death of their own race. This is what they wanted to kill in the bodies of Jews and all others who seemed to threaten from within and without. Furthermore, they considered that infected life dead already. Thus, the Nazis did not see their actions as actual murder. They merely reestablished the rights of life by restoring an already dead life to death, giving death to a life that had always been inhabited and corrupted by death. They made death, rather than life, both the therapeutic object and the therapeutic instrument. This explains why they always had a cult of their own ancestors— because, in a biopolitical perspective that had been completely turned into thanatopolitics—only death could have the role of defending life from itself, by making all life submit to the regime of death. The fifty million deaths produced by the Second World War represent the inevitable outcome of such logic.

Nevertheless, this catastrophe did not spell the end of biopolitics, which corroborates what I noted above—namely that, in its various configurations, biopolitics has a history that is much vaster and older than Nazism, even though Nazism would appear to carry biopolitics to its extreme. Biopolitics is not a product of Nazism; if anything, Nazism is the paroxysmal and degenerated product of a certain kind of biopolitics. This is a point that's worth remembering, because biopolitics can cause, and has caused, numerous misunderstandings. Contrary to the illusions of those who imagined it was possible to retroactively skip over what for them amounted to the Nazi parenthesis so as to reconstruct the governing principles of the preceding period, life and politics are bound together in a knot that can't be undone. The period of peace (at least in the Western world) that followed the Second World War nourished this illusion. The fact that even the peace— or rather nonwar, as was the case for the Cold War—that followed was founded upon a balance of terror underpinned by the atomic bomb, and therefore fell entirely within an immunitary logic, mattered little. All it did was defer by a few decades what would have happened sooner or later. Indeed the collapse of the Soviet system, which some interpreted as the final victory of democracy over its potential enemies, if not the end of history itself, marked instead the end of that illusion. The knot binding politics and life together, which totalitarianism tightened with destructive consequences for both, is still before our eyes. We might even say that this knot has become the very epicenter of every politically significant dynamic. We see it in the increasing importance of ethnicity in international relations to the impact of biotechnologies on the human body, from the centrality of health care as the most important index of how efficient economic-productive systems are to the priority that security measures enjoy in all government programs. Politics seems to be more and more made one with the bare ground of biology, if not with the very body of citizens in every part of the world. The increasing indistinction between norm and exception that results from indiscriminantly extending emergency legislation, together with the growing influx of migrants stripped of all juridical identity and subjected to direct screening by the police, marks an additional step in the biopolitical. We really ought to reflect on these world events outside the context of globalization. One might even say that, contrary to what Heidegger and Hannah Arendt believed with their respective differences, the question of life cannot be separated from that of the world. The philosophical idea (coming to us from phenomenology) of the "life-world" is thus over-turned symmetrically to become "world-life," by which I mean that the entire world seems increasingly to be a body united by a single global threat that holds it together and at the same time risks smashing it to pieces. Unlike previous periods, no longer can one part of the world (America, Europe) be saved while another self-destructs. A single destiny binds the world, the whole world, and its life. Either the world will find a way to survive together, or it will perish as one.

The events set in motion by the terrorist attacks of September 11, 2001 do not constitute, as many argued, the beginning but instead the detonation of a process that started with the end of the Soviet system, which was the last *katechon* inhibiting the world's self-destructive urges, thanks to the vice of reciprocal fear. Here, when this last wall that had given the world a dual form came to an end, biopolitical dynamics no longer seemed capable of being halted or contained. The war in Iraq signals the height of this drift of the biopolitical, given both the motivations for starting it and for how the war was and is still being carried out. The idea of a preventive war radically shifts the terms of the debate with respect to both wars waged and the so-called Cold War. For the latter, it is as if the negative part of the immunitary procedure is multiplied to such a degree that it occupies the entire frame. War thus becomes no longer the exception, a last resort, or the ever-present opposite of existence but the sole form of global coexistence, the constitutive category of existence today. Not surprisingly, the consequence is a disproportionate multiplication of the very risks that we wanted to avoid. The most obvious result is the complete superimposition of opposites: peace and war, attack and defense, life and death, in which each weighs more and more on the other.

If we pause to look more closely at the homicidal and suicidal logic of terrorist practices today, we quickly see an additional step with respect to Nazi thanatopolitics. No longer does only death make a dramatic entrance into life, but now life itself is constituted as death's instrument. What is a kamikaze, truly, if not a fragment of life hurled upon other lives in order to produce death? And don't terrorist attacks aim ever more at women and children, the very sources of life? The barbarism of decapitating hostages seems to bring us back to the premodern age of punishments in the public square, with a touch of the hypermodern constituted by the planetary Internet booths where we can see such a spectacle. The virtual, which is anything but in opposition to the real, constitutes here the real's most concrete manifestation in the very body of the victims and in the blood that seems to spurt onto the screen. Today, as never before, politics is practiced on the bodies, in the bodies, of unarmed and innocent victims. Yet even more significant in the current biopolitical drift is that the prevention of mass terror itself tends to absorb and reproduce the very modalities of terror. How else are we to read tragic episodes like the massacre that took place at the Dubrovka Theater in Moscow, where the police used lethal gas on both terrorists and hostages? And isn't the torture that is widely practiced in Iraqi prisons a perfect example of politics acting on life [*politica sulla vita*], halfway between the incision of the condemned's body in Kafka's "In the Penal Colony" and the beastialization of the enemy that comes to us from the Nazis?[10] The fact that in the recent Afghanistan war the same airplanes dropped bombs and food rations on the same populations is perhaps the most tangible sign of the nearly complete identity between the defense of life and the production of death.

Is this how biopolitical discourse ends? Is the only possible outcome of such events such an overlapping, or is there another way of practicing, or at least thinking, biopolitics, which is to say a biopolitics that is ultimately affirmative, productive, and removed from death's nonstop presence? In other words, is a politics no longer *over* life [*sulla vita*] but *of* life [*della vita*] imaginable? If it is, then how should it, how might it, take shape? First, a clarification. Despite the legitimacy of political philosophy as an area of study, I'm wary of any easy short circuit between philosophy and politics. Their co-implication cannot be resolved by looking to a complete superimposition; I don't believe that philosophy's task is to offer models of political institutions or that, conversely, biopolitics can become a revolutionary or, depending on your taste, reformist manifesto. My feeling is that a much longer and clearer path is needed, one that includes a decidedly philosophical effort toward a new conceptual elaboration. If, as Deleuze believes, philosophy is the practice of creating appropriate concepts for the event that touches and transforms us, this is the moment to rethink the relationship between politics and life in a way that, instead of making life subject to the direction of politics, as took place over the course of the last century, we ought to introduce the power [*potenza*] of life into politics.[11] The key is relating to biopolitics not from outside but from within biopolitics, until we are able to bring something to the surface that until today has been crushed by its opposite. We have no recourse except to refer to this opposite if only so as to establish a starting point through contrast. In *Bíos*, I chose the most difficult path, at whose beginning is the site of the most extreme and lethal drift of biopolitics (Nazism) and its thanatopolitical *dispositifs*. I began my search there from within these paradigms in search of the keys for the doors opening to a different politics of life. I realize how vexing this might sound to some, attempting to employ such a contrast using a common sense term that for a long period has attempted, consciously or unconsciously, to dismiss the question of Nazism, or of what Nazism understood and unfortunately practiced as the politics of the *bíos* (even though, having recourse to the Aristotelian vocabulary, we ought in this case to speak of *zoé*). The three lethal apparatuses of Nazism that I've worked on are the absolute normalization of life, or the imprisonment of *bíos* within the law of its own destruction; the double enclosure of the body, or the homicidal and suicidal immunization of the German people within the figure of a single, racially purified body; and, finally, the suppression of birth in advance, as a way of cancelling life at the very moment of its emergence. To these apparatuses I contrasted not something from the outside but their exact opposite: a conception of a norm that is immanent to bodies, not imposed upon them from outside, a break with the closed and organic idea of a political body in favor of the multiplicity of "flesh of the world," and finally a politics of birth understood as the continual production of difference in terms of identity. Without wanting to discuss these areas again in detail, I orient them toward an unprecedented joining of a language of life and a political form through philosophical reflection. How much all of this can carry us forward toward an affirmative biopolitics is still anyone's guess. What interested me was highlighting the traces, unraveling some of the threads, and shedding light on some of the darker areas that might help us glimpse something that we still can't make out clearly.

NAZISM AND US

1933–2003. Is it legitimate to turn once again to the question of Nazism seventy years after it took power? The answer, I believe, can only be yes: not just because forgetting Nazism would represent an unbearable offense for its victims but also because, despite an ever increasing body of literature, something about Nazism remains in the dark, something that touches us. What might it be? What links us invisibly to what we point to as the most tragic political catastrophe of our time, and perhaps of all time? My own sense is that this thing that both troubles and evades us remains locked up within the concept of totalitarianism. Naturally, we know how much this concept, especially in Hannah Arendt's formulation, has helped shed light on the radical turn that took place in the 1920s in the institutional, political and ethical order of the preceding era.[1] And yet the very concept of totalitarianism ends up eliding, or at least shading over, the specificity of the Nazi event with respect to other experiences relegated to the same category—above all, that of Soviet communism. Clearly this does not mean that nothing crosscuts the two phenomena: mass society, constructivist violence, generalized terror, and so forth. But this all-too-obvious link does not reach the deepest layer of Nazism that's inassimilable to every other event of the near or remote past.

From such a perspective, a profound difference between the two "totalitarianisms" is revealed in their relationships to what we call modernity: While communist totalitarianism, even in its typicality, springs forth from modernity's womb—that is, from within its own logics, dynamics, and drifts—the Nazi variant signals a drastic change of course. It is born not from a carrying to the extreme but from a decomposition of the modern form. This is not because Nazism doesn't contain elements, fragments, or shards of modernity but because Nazism restores or translates them into an absolutely new conceptual language that is completely irreducible to the political, social, and anthropological parameters of the previous, modern lexicon. If one can always say that communism "realizes" a philosophical tradition that belongs to modernity in some (however exasperated and extreme) way, it's in no way possible to say the same about Nazism. Therefore, even more than other, more contingent incompatibilities, Nazism's encounter with Heidegger's philosophy swiftly proved itself to be a terrible misunderstanding for both. But precisely because Nazism lies entirely outside of modern language, because it is situated decidedly *after* it, Nazism embarrassingly brushes up against a dimension that is part of our experience as postmoderns. Contrary to what certain common-sense speech declares, we are operating no longer within the reverse side [*rovescio*] of communism but within that of Nazism. This is our *question*, the monster that stalks us not only from behind but also from our future.

How so? We've said that Nazism is not philosophy realized as is communism. But this is only a half truth that we should complete as follows: It is actually *biology* realized. If communism has history as its transcendental, class as its subject, and economy as its lexicon, Nazism has life as its transcendental, race as its subject, and biology as its lexicon. Certainly, communists also maintained that they were acting according to a precise scientific vision, but only Nazis identified that science as the comparative biology of human races. From this perspective, we must accept Rudolph Hess's declarations that "National Socialism is nothing but applied biology."[2] Actually, the expression was used for the first time by the geneticist Fritz Lenz in the widely circulated *Rassenhygiene* manual (written alongside Erwin Baur and Eugen Fischer)—a text in which Hitler was defined as "the great German doctor" capable of carrying out "the final step in the defeat of historicism and in the recognition of purely biological values."[3] Furthermore, Hitler himself had declared in *Mein Kampf* that "if the power to fight for one's own health is no longer present, the right to live in this world of struggle ends."[4] In another influential medical text, Rudolph Ramm named the "physician of the *Volk*" a "biological soldier" in the service of the "great idea of the of the National Socialist biological state structure."[5] Medical power and military power [*potere*] refer to one another, added Kurt Blome (deputy to Reich Health Leader Leonardo Conti) in his 1942 *Arzt im Kampf* [*Physi-*

cian in Struggle]—because both are engaged in the final battle for the life of the Reich.

We must be careful not to lose sight of the specific quality of the biological, and more specifically medical, semantics deployed by the Nazis. Interpreting politics in biomedical terms, and, inversely, attributing political significance to biomedicine meant placing oneself on a radically different horizon from that of the entire modern tradition because, in Ramm's words, "National Socialism, differently from any other political philosophy or party program, aligns itself with natural history and human biology."[6] It's true that the political lexicon uses and incorporates biological metaphors, beginning with the long-standing one of the state-body. And it's also true, as Foucault has brought to light, that beginning in the eighteenth century the question of life progressively intersected more and more with the sphere of political action. The same ideas of *National-Biologie* or *biologische Politik* are rooted in the culture of the German Empire and the Weimar Republic.[7] Yet we have before us a phenomenon that's quite different in both scope and significance. In a certain way, the metaphor becomes real—not in the sense that political power is given directly to doctors and biologists (although this did happen in more than one case)—but in the more urgent sense that political officials assumed a medical-biological principle as the guiding criteria of their actions. We are therefore not talking about mere instrumentalization: Nazi politics was not limited to wielding the biomedical research of the times to legitimate itself; rather, the former attempted to identify itself directly with latter.[8] When Hans Reiter, speaking in the name of the Reich of occupied Paris, declared that "this way of thinking in biological terms must eventually be adopted by the entire people," because with them the "substance" of the very "body of the nation" was at stake, he was well aware that he was speaking in the name of something that had never been part of modern conceptual language. This is why today, even in the twilight of modernity, we are directly implicated.[9]

Only in this way can we explain the tight web that was woven over the course of those horrifying twelve years between politics, law, and medicine, whose final outcome was genocide. Certainly, the participation of the medical class in thanatopolitical practice was a characteristic not only of Nazism. We all know the role of psychiatrists in diagnosing dissidents with mental illness in the Gulags of the Soviet Union, as well as the role of Japanese doctors who performed vivisections on American prisoners. Still, in

Germany the situation was different. Here, I'm not only speaking about the experiments on "human guinea pigs" or about the collections of Jewish skulls sent directly from the camps to anthropological institutes. We know about the generous anatomic gifts sent from Mengele to his teacher Otmar von Verschuer, who is still considered one of the founders of modern genetics. We've even witnessed the verdict of a tribunal, and the institution of the Nuremburg Code protecting human subjects, which came out of the trial of the doctors who were held directly responsible for murder.[10] But the paltry sentences in relation to the enormity of the act testifies to the fact that the problem was not so much determining the individual responsibility of doctors (which would have been inevitable) but defining the overall role medicine played in Nazi ideology and practice. Why was medicine the profession that, more than any other, supported the regime so unconditionally? And why did the regime grant doctors such an extensive power over life and death? Why did it seem to hand the physician the sovereign's scepter and, before that, the clergyman's book?

When Gerhard Wagner, führer of German doctors before Leonardo Conti, said that the physician, "should go back to his origins, he should again be a priest, he should become priest and physician in one," he simply affirms that ultimately only the physician reserves the right to judge who is to be kept alive and who will be condemned to death.[11] The physician alone possesses the definition of valid life, a valued life, and therefore only he can set the limits beyond which life can legitimately be extinguished. The many doctors valorized by the regime did not hesitate to accept its mandates and to carry them out with swift efficiency: from the selection of children and then of adults destined for the "merciful death" of the T4 program to the extension of what was continually called "euthanasia" to prisoners of war (the 14f13 project), to the enormous *Therapia magna auschwitzciense*—the selection on the ramp leading into the camp, the start of the process of gassing, the declaration of death [*decesso*], the extraction of gold teeth from cadavers, and the overseeing of cremation. No step in the production of death escaped their control. According to the precise instructions issued by Viktor Brack, head of the Euthanasia Department of the Reich Chancellery, only physicians had the right to inject phenol into the hearts of "degenerates" or to open the gas valve for the final "shower." If ultimate power wore the boots of the SS, *auctoritas* wore the white coat of the doctor. Even the cars that transported Zyklon B to Birkenau bore the sign of the Red

Cross and the inscription that stood out at the entrance to Mathausen was "Cleanliness and Health." In the no-man's-land of this new theo-bio-politics, physicians had truly become once again the priests of Baal, who after millennia found themselves before their ancient Jewish enemies and could devour them at will. It's been widely noted that Auschwitz-Birkenau was the world's largest genetics laboratory.[12]

We also know that the Reich knew how to generously compensate its doctors—not only with professorships and honors but with something even more concrete. If Conti reported directly to Himmler, the surgeon Karl Brandt, who had already been charged with the euthanasia operation, became one of the regime's most powerful officers. His limitless jurisdiction included the life and death of all and he was subject only to the supreme authority of the Führer. Not to mention Irmfried Eberl, who was "promoted" at thirty-two to commander of Treblinka. Does this mean that all German physicians, or even only those who supported Nazism, consciously sold their souls to the devil? Were they simply butchers in white coats? Although it may be convenient to think so, this wasn't necessarily the case. Not only was German medical research among the most advanced in the world (Wilhelm Hueper, the father of professional American carcinogenesis, asked the Nazi minister of culture Bernhard Rust to return to work in the "new Germany") but Nazis launched the most powerful campaign of the period against cancer by restricting the use of asbestos, tobacco, pesticides, and colorants, encouraging the distribution of organic and vegetarian foods, and alerting people to the potentially carcinogenic effects of X-rays (which they used in the meantime to sterilize women who weren't worth the cost of a salpingectomy). At Dachau, while the chimney smoked, organic honey was being produced. Moreover, Hitler himself detested smoking, and was a vegetarian and animal lover besides being scrupulously attentive to hygiene.[13]

What does all of this decidedly obsessive attention to public health (which had significant effects on the death-from-cancer rate in Germany) suggest? Between this therapeutic attitude and the thanatological frame in which it is inscribed, there was not only a contradiction but a profound connection. Insofar as doctors were obsessively preoccupied with the health of the German body, doctors made a deadly incision (in the surgical sense) in the flesh of that body. In short, though it may seem tragically paradoxical, German doctors became executioners of those they considered inessential or harmful to the improvement of public health in order to carry out their therapeutic mission. From this point of view, we are compelled to argue that genocide was the result of not the absence but the presence of a medical ethics that was perverted into its opposite. It does not suffice to say that in the biomedical vision of Nazism the border between healing and murder was breached. We must instead conceive of them as two sides of the same project, which made one the necessary condition of the other: Only by murdering as many people as possible could they heal those who represented the true Germany. From this perspective, it even appears plausible that at least some Nazi physicians truly believed they were respecting in content, if not in form, the Hippocratic oath to do no harm to the patient. Yet they identified the patient as, rather than a single individual, the German people as a whole. Caring for the German people required the mass death of all those who threatened its health by simply existing. In this sense, we ought to defend the claim I advanced earlier that Nazism's transcendental is life, rather than death—even if, paradoxically, death was considered the only medicine capable of conserving life. "The Nazi message—for victims, for possible observers, and mostly for themselves—was: all our killing is medical, medically indicated, and carried out by doctors."[14] With Telegram 71, in which Hitler ordered, from his Berlin bunker, the destruction of the means of subsistence of the German people who had shown their weakness, the limit point of the Nazi antinomy suddenly became clear: The life of some, and ultimately of one, is sanctioned only by the death of everyone.[15]

We know that Michel Foucault interpreted this thanatopolitical dialectic in terms of biopolitics: As soon as power [potere] takes up life itself as an object of calculation and an instrument for its own ends, it becomes possible, at least in certain conditions, for power to decide to sacrifice one part of the population to benefit another.[16] Without undermining the importance of Foucault's reading, I don't believe it explains everything. Why did Nazism, unlike all other forms of power past and present, push this homicidal possibility to its fullest realization? Why did it, and only it, reverse the proportion between life and death in favor of the latter, to the point of planning its own self-destruction? I suggest that the category of biopolitics must be merged with that of immunization. Only immunization lays bare the lethal knot that thrusts the protection of life toward its potential negation. Furthermore, through the figure of autoimmune disease, the category of immunization identifies the threshold beyond which the protective apparatus attacks the very body that it should protect.[17] Moreover, the fact that the sickness from which Nazism intended to defend the German people wasn't just any disease but an infectious disease illustrates that immunization is the interpretative key most apt for understanding the specificity of Nazism. What Nazism wanted to avoid at all costs was the contagion of superior beings by inferior beings. The deadly battle that was waged and disseminated by the regime's propaganda placed the originally healthy body and blood of the German nation in opposition to the invasive germs that had penetrated the nation with the intent of sapping its unity and its very life. The repertoire that the Reich's ideologues employed to portray their alleged enemies and most of all the Jews is well known: They were, at once, "bacilli," "bacteria," "viruses," "parasites," and "microbes." Andrzej Kaminski recalls that even interned Soviets were at times defined in similar terms.[18] Moreover, characterizing Jews as parasites is part of the secular history of (not exclusively) German anti-Judaism. Still, in the Nazi vocabulary, such a definition acquires a different meaning. It was as if something that had remained up to a certain point a loaded metaphor actually took on a physical shape [corpo]. This is the effect of the total biologization of the lexicon I referred to above: Jews do not *resemble* parasites, they do not behave *like* bacteria—they *are* such things. And they are treated as such. Thus the correct term for their massacre, which is anything but a sacred "holocaust," is *extermination*: something that is carried out against insects, rats, or lice. In this way, we must ascribe an entirely literal meaning to Himmler's words to the SS officers at Kharkov that "anti-Semitism is like a disinfestation. Removing lice is not an ideological question, but a question of hygiene [pulizia]."[19] Moreover, Hitler himself used even more precise immunological terminology: "The discovery of the Jewish virus is one of the great revolutions of this world. The battle in which we are engaged today is of the same sort as the battle waged, during the last century, by Pasteur and Koch . . . We shall regain our health only by eliminating the Jews."[20]

We ought not blur the difference between this approach, which is bacteriological, and one that is simply racial. The final solution waged against the Jews has precisely such a biological-immunitarian characterization. Even the gas used in the camps flowed through shower pipes that were used for disinfection; but disinfecting Jews was impossible, because they were the bacteria from which one needed to rid oneself. The identification between man and pathogens reached such a point that the Warsaw ghetto was intentionally built on an already contaminated site. In this way, like a

self-fulfilling prophecy, Jews fell victim to the same sickness that had justi-
fied their ghettoization: Finally, they had *really* become infected and thus
agents of infection.[21] Doctors therefore had good reason to exterminate
them. Naturally, this representation was in patent contrast with the Men-
delian theory of the genetic, and therefore not contagious, character of racial
determination. For precisely this reason, the only way to stop the impossible contagion seemed to be to eliminate all of its possible carriers, and not
only them but also all Germans who may have already been contaminated,
as well as all those who may have eventually been so in the future, and, once
the war was lost and the Russians were a few kilometers from Hitler's bunker, quite simply *everyone*. Here the immunitary paradigm of Nazi biopolitics reaches the height of its auto-genocidal fury. As in the most devastating
autoimmune disease, the defensive potential of the immune system turns
against itself. The only possible outcome is generalized destruction.

What about us? The sixty years that separate us from the end of those
tragic events form a barrier that nevertheless appears difficult to overcome.
It's truly difficult to imagine that it could happen again, at least in the ever-
larger space that we still call the West. We wouldn't be theorists of immunization if we thought that the twelve-year Nazi experience failed to produce
sufficient antibodies to protect us from its return. Still, such common sense
rationalizations aren't able to bring to a close a discourse that, as we've said,
remains with us. I'd even add that not only is the problem, or the terrifying
laceration, opened by Nazism anything but definitively healed but, in a
certain way, it seems to come closer to our condition the more our condition exceeds the confines of modernity. We might best measure the enduring relevance of Nazism's foundational presuppositions from the vantage
point of the final collapse of Soviet communism. The relationship between
the two is far from casual: The definitive consummation of the communist
philosophy of history that favored the reemergence of the question of life
was, after all, at the heart of Nazi semantics. Furthermore, never as today has
bíos, if not *zoé*, been the point of intersection for all political, social, economic, and technological practices. This is why, once the conceptual lexicon (if not the political exigency) of communism was worn out, we turned
to reckon with that of Nazism, only to find it stamped across our foreheads.
Whoever deluded him- or herself at the end of the war, or even in the post-
war era, into thinking it was possible to reactivate the old categories of the
democracies who emerged as the official winners of the battle got it all

wrong. It's utopian to argue that the complexity of the globalized world, with its sharp imbalances in wealth, power, and demographic density, can be governed with the ineffectual instruments of international law or with those left over from the traditional sovereign powers. To do so would be to fail to understand that we're approaching a threshold that's just as dramatic as the one that separated the 1920s and 1930s. Just as then, though in a different way, the soldering of politics to life makes all of the traditional theoretical and institutional categories, beginning with that of representation, irrelevant. A glance at the panorama that inaugurates the beginning of the twenty-first century is enough to give us a striking picture: from the explosion of biological terrorism to the preventative war that attempts to respond to it on its own terrain, from ethnic—that is, biological—massacres to the mass migrations that sweep away the barriers that are intended to contain them, from technologies that invest not only individual bodies but also the traits of the species to psychopharmacology that modifies our vital behaviors, from environmental politics to the explosion of new epidemics, from the reopening of concentration camps in different areas of the world to the blurring of the juridical distinction between norm and exception—all of this while everywhere a new and potentially devastating immunitary syndrome breaks out once again, uncontrollably. As we've said, none of this replicates what happened from 1933 to 1945. But nothing is entirely external to the questions of life and death that were posed then. To say that we are, now more than ever, on the reverse side of Nazism means that it isn't possible to rid ourselves of it by simply averting our gaze. To truly overturn it, to throw it back into the hell whence it came, we must consciously cross through that darkness once again and respond quite differently to the same questions that gave rise to it.

POLITICS AND HUMAN NATURE

The "Letter on Humanism" that Martin Heidegger published in 1946 at the culmination of an historical and biographic defeat seems to spell the end of the secular event of humanism. Despite the attempts to restore humanism to a spiritualist, Marxist, or existentialist form, the great humanist tradition could not withstand the dual trauma of Auschwitz and Hiroshima, in which the opposite of humanity laid waste to the very idea of humanity.[1] Regardless of the direct and even instrumental conditions that underpin the drafting of the "Letter," the need of such an epistemological break is central to Heidegger's text: a culture of man that did not know how to avoid, and perhaps even fostered, the mass murder of fifty million people in the heart of the twentieth century cannot imagine that it will survive. The idea that after a catastrophe of such dimensions it would be possible to restore the old-style humanist myth of man as the ruler of his own destiny is doomed for at least two reasons: first, because it's impossible to send history back in time toward a definitively past-tense moment and, second, because the smoking rubble dominating the symbolic and material field after the war has its origins in precisely such a past.

Yet if Heidegger's "Letter" signals a point of no return vis-à-vis everything understood by the idea *humanitas* for at least five centuries, we can't actually say that the essay casts *humanitas* in a language that is truly innovative. The reason isn't only because of Heidegger's temporary compromise with antihuman powers [*potenze*] but for a more important reason that has to do with his very definition of "humanity." Without losing ourselves in the particular details, let's simply say that Heidegger's detachment with respect to the humanist tradition (which he weaves together with a thread connecting the Greek *paideia* to *romanitas*, up through the modern *studia humanitatis*) keeps him within the same semantic orbit. Moreover, he himself spoke of the need to think against humanism because "it does not set the *humanitas* of man high enough."[2] What did Heidegger mean by that? In what sense would humanism have betrayed itself by placing man in an inferior position with respect to its deepest meaning? The philosopher's response is well known: Humanism didn't know how to free itself from the metaphysical lexicon because it "thinks of man on the basis of *animalitas* and does not think in the direction of his *humanitas*."[3] Humanism understands man as an animal species, one that is certainly unique insofar as he is endowed with the charisma of reason. Yet he's not essentially different from other species. Whichever name is conferred upon him, man continues to be conceived of as an *animal rationale*: "In principle we are still thinking of *homo animalis*—even when *anima* [soul] is posited as *animus sive mens* [spirit or mind], and this in turn is later posited as subject, person, or spirit [*Geist*]."[4] For Heidegger, this was the fatal error that caused humanism first to contradict itself and then to turn against itself: not the search for a human essence that preceded its existence, as Sartre would claim, but that essence's lack of distinction, and even its derivation, from a not-exactly-human living material. The beastialization of man tried out in the Nazi extermination camps would be rooted in the categorical confusion between man and animal, which the humanistic category of *humanitas* described from the very outset.

This indistinction, or marriage, between animality and rationality distances humanism's man from that privileged relationship with the sphere of being [*essere*], which can be identified only by the element that radically separates humankind from any other living being, which is to say language. To claim that language makes man *man* means, for Heidegger, defining him first and foremost with regard to man's contrast with the silence of animals. Yet, precisely for this reason, it also means moving outside from his definition that phenomenon of simple life that connects all living beings in a singular biological dimension. Once he has pivoted (toward removing man, or at least the ultimate truth of man, from the realm of life), Heidegger can then hypothesize that "the essence of divinity is closer to us than what is so alien in other living creatures."[5] Notwithstanding his precocious interest in "factical life" (which he exhibited during his Freiburg courses in the 1920s), and despite some curiosity about medicine and psychiatry (to which the Zollikon Seminars attest), one might say that the gaping void set out by Heidegger between man and animal is the same one that keeps his philosophy some distance not only from what the Greeks called *zoé*, or simple life, but also from the entire horizon of *bíos*. That the animal is subsequently defined as "poor in world," in opposition to man as "world-forming," is another way of marking the interval that, in the *Dasein*, separates the sphere of being-in-the-world from that of biological life. Moreover, and this is true even in *Being and Time*, what makes man worthy of such a name is not life, which is present in every other inferior organism, but if anything death. Unlike man, these organisms endure death unwittingly. More than living, man is essentially mortal: the being-toward-death. This is what Heidegger makes the center of his own ontology, in contrast with the humanist tradition, and at the same time with every positive body of knowledge about life. His thesis is that, in order to grasp human reality more deeply than humanism ever could, one must think the human outside of the shared horizon of something that merely lives. The truth of man resides, for Heidegger, beyond, or before, his simple life, which Heidegger's not insubstantial disinterest in the body demonstrates. This is why, notwithstanding his desire to address his meditation, "not only [to] man, but [to] the 'nature' of man," Heidegger excludes from that nature of man every reference to the biological; on the contrary, he finds in such an exclusion the road that leads to that more primordial realm "in which the essence of man, determined by Being itself, is at home."[6]

Did Heidegger actually manage to free himself from the humanist tradition that he wants to critique? Does he speak a language utterly distinct from that of classical humanism? It's difficult to say yes to either question. Certainly, the decentering of the human entity in relation to the dimension of being around which all of Heidegger's thought is constructed is all too evident. So too his deconstruction of subjectivist and objectivist metaphysics, which gives man ownership of himself and all that surrounds him, is also clear. *Dasein* is not the man of humanism, if only because man is constitutively cut by a difference from himself that makes him unstable. Yet all of this occurs in a modality that, rather than arguing against man's absolute uniqueness and difference with regard to all other living beings, confirms and deepens such difference in such a way that Heidegger's thought resembles traditional anthropodicy. Once abandoned by God to his worldly destiny, Heidegger's existing being inherits not only God's absoluteness but also his primacy over all other species, from whom he is separated not by a different nature but by his structural lack. Man's essence lies more in his extraneousness to the natural realm than in his belonging to a specific nature. Here, that conceptual dichotomy between natural sciences and knowledge of man that Heidegger also attempted to overcome by employing a different conceptual lexicon takes root and intensifies. The natural sciences cannot make out the reality of man—that is, existence—because man does not have, in the proper sense, a nature, or because his nature is fundamentally unnatural. If anything, man has a "condition," as Hannah Arendt will say (from a different point of view) in *The Human Condition*. There she shares the antibiologistic prejudice of her teacher: Life is the biological presupposition from which human existence must separate itself in order to assume the anthropological, political, or philosophical meaning that belongs to it. But it is just such an antinaturalistic prejudice that keeps Heidegger's *humanitas* in close proximity to the very humanistic tradition à la Pico that it would like to surpass. Wasn't it Pico who kept *dignitas humana* at a distance from every natural given? And didn't he also find the difference, even the superiority, of man over other animals in just such a condition? While other animals are granted a fixed nature by God and bound inexorably to a natural environment (as twentieth-century philosophical anthropology will later tell us), man, and only man, has no permanent place in the world, and, precisely for this reason, he may choose one to his liking. Thus, as he is free to decline toward lesser beings or to rise to the heights of divine ones, man is capable of transforming himself continually. "Man fashions, fabricates, and transforms himself" (*Fingit, fabricat et transformat se ipsum*) at will.[7] No ontological fetters, permanent characteristics, or natural invariables tie him to a specific natural modality. He is nothing, because he can become everything, create himself again and again whenever he pleases. Properly speaking, he is not even a being but a becoming in perpetual transformation.

When, four centuries later, Sartre writes (with the air of someone setting forth a radically new framework) that, "man is free and there is no human nature in which I can place my trust," he merely recommends again the idea that first gave rise to the humanist tradition.[8] He does so, of course, from a vantage point that puts the plane of existence before essence, by restoring existence to the very antinatural realm through which the humanist tradition had thought essence. One need only replace the term *essence* with *nature* to see where the two positions, which are different only in principle, actually converge. Writing, as Sartre does, that "man is nothing other than what he makes himself" means situating him in a radically historical dimension that is thus removed from any natural basis.[9] True, man is always finite, but for this reason he also infinitely creates himself. Man is the subject of his own substance, which continually is dissolved into his own subjectivity. The grafting of Marxist motifs onto such a phenomenological frame does not alter the terms of the discourse much. Nature, more than a biological component of the human subject, is considered to be the material instrument of his historic autoproduction. When Sartre insists that, for existentialism, man is always outside of himself, poised for a continual transcendence of his natural condition, we must take him literally. Although man is integrated into a series of material conditions that come before him, man tests his own authentic humanity at the very point in which he detaches himself from that humanity, in order to fashion himself according to his own existential decision. His nature is only of interest insofar as it is to be overcome. Subjected to wholesale historicization, existence winds up radically distancing itself from that life. Or perhaps life takes on a human character only by removing itself from its biological meaning. If with respect to philosophical terminology Heidegger clearly distances himself from such a semantics (insofar as he deconstructs all of its concepts—that is, from the subject to substance, from nature to history), when it comes to the relationship between *humanitas* and *bíos*, he remains fundamentally within its borders. The very temporal qualification of *Dasein*, which takes apart every complete image of subjectivity, follows the same antinaturalistic course. More than truly abandoned, humanistic discourse appears dialectically integrated within, or subsumed and overcome by, an additional configuration. None of its basic presuppositions—namely, the refusal of biological notions of human nature, the absolute opposition between man and other living species, the underestimation of the body as the primary dimension of existence—is actually put up for discussion. Behind the critique of humanism, the ancient outline of *man* as *humanus* reappears.

There's yet another reason why Heidegger doesn't inaugurate a new, posthumanist language, and it is because such a language did not wait for his "Letter" to appear. First Darwin and then Nietzsche used such language, when they were not busy inventing it. They did so in quite distinct ways, such that the latter bitterly critiqued the former (whom he only knew secondhand

and fundamentally misunderstood). What Nietzsche criticized was Spencer's simplified interpretation of Darwin, which Nietzsche erroneously identified with the positivistic doctrine of progress. One might even say that the richest meaning of the Darwinian perspective lies in its deconstruction of the teleological and essentialist progressivism that the humanist tradition had assumed and elaborated. Without lingering any longer than is necessary on the general arrangement of Darwin's theory of evolution, there are two, naturally interwoven, points in which his break with the humanist lexicon is most clear: On the one hand, Darwin replaces the search for man's essence, or condition, with a search for his nature (defined according to a series of biological invariants). On the other hand, Darwin places man, notwithstanding all of his proper and peculiar features, within a general chain of living species. This means that Darwin neither reduces human behavior to a mere reflex of man's organic composition nor opposes nature to history as something stable and permanent. On the contrary, he integrates the two according to a concept of natural history that involves the modification of human nature on the basis of a series of deviations from the norm that cannot be made out in advance but produced spontaneously and randomly. The mechanism of natural selection works precisely on these variations—this is the third, and most important, point of departure from the humanist tradition: Human nature is not a unified entity that progresses, but the ever-alterable result of an endless conflict between different biological typologies that compete for prominence.

We know that this last principle is what Nietzsche assumed and which he carried to its most extreme. Still, this is not the place to track his discourse in all of its infinite folds, nuances, and contradictions. At its core, however, surely lies an awareness of the inadequacy of European humanism, which he defines as nihilism precisely insofar as it repeatedly attempts to reinvigorate its own depleted values with what seems to him as *the* demand of his own (and of our) time: not only the scientific, philosophical, and political centrality of *bíos* as a whole, with all of its thresholds, but also the battle that is waged about the methods and outcomes of *bíos*'s transformation. What Nietzsche sees with a clearness of perspective that sets him above any other thinker of his time is that behind, and within, the classic question of *humanitas* a conflict has broken out whose ultimate stake has to do with the very definition of man, and with what man might become as soon as the issue of modifying his makeup is raised. Clearly Nietzsche takes up the ancient Pichian myth of human plasticity—that is, man's production of his own essence. At the same time, Nietzsche translates the myth into biological terms when he makes the object of this transformation not the soul or the social condition but man's very body, or, better still, man as a bio-determined entity in which soul, condition, and body constitute a single living organism.

Naturally, this presents some risks. As soon as the anthrotechnological (or, as I prefer, biopolitical) vector of artificial intervention in human nature meets the other Darwinian presupposition of nearness to the animal world, which itself contains social or even ethnoracial terms, the consequences can be disastrous. When Nietzsche asks himself, "why shouldn't we be able to accomplish with human beings what the Chinese have learned to do with trees—that it carries roses on one side and pears on the other?" not only is he theorizing the move from Darwinian natural selection to a project of artificial selection but he also imagines an anthropological structure in which humankind is divided into nonequivalent categories of those who are selected and those who do the selecting.[10] Indeed, this comparison between plants and animals, which he pushes forward in other texts, drifts ideologically, assigning one group of humankind to an inferior living species, which is necessary for the dominion of those who are destined to perform better. Even here, Nietzsche uses the Pichian motif of the oscillation of the human being between degeneration toward animality and regeneration toward divinity. The difference is that rather than constituting the polarities between which humankind moves back and forth, the two conditions—that is, the animal and divine—become anthropic typologies internal to it. The move from here to the beastialization of a certain kind of man and the making divine of another, which had the most extreme and fatal thanatological consequences in the decades that followed, is neither impossible nor unforeseeable. Obviously this doesn't mean making Nietzsche responsible for a result for which his thought can in no way be held accountable (as the very people who arbitrarily claimed his legacy attempted to do). Terms such as *domestication* (*Zähmung*) and *breeding* (*Züchtung*), referring to men who are selected for such ends, certainly do open up a way into the old notion of *humanitas*, through which anything may pass. That drive toward the "domestication" of man with regard to his originally feral tendencies, which a long and illustrious tradition running from Erasmus to Goethe had conceived of in terms of spiritual education and formation is now reinterpreted in anthropo- and zootechnological terms. Furthermore, as noted earlier, what happened in Nazi Germany is not entirely foreign to the basis of the humanist and anthropocentric *ratio*, which has characterized it since its inception. As the extraordinary development of the German anthropology of the time (which was never detached from but instead ran parallel to and crossed paths with zoology) reveals, Nazis never actually gave up on the category of *humanitas*—so much so that various racial hygiene manuals had *humanitas* as their title. Weren't they attempting to improve humankind by immunizing it from its contaminating waste? Rather than directly making man into beast, Nazism effectively widened the definition of *anthropos* to the point of including within it even animals of inferior species. He who is the object of extreme violence wasn't simply similar to animals. He was an animal-man: an animal with the face of man, or a man inhabited by an animal.

Is this destructive and self-destructive face the only one post-humanism can put on? Is it a given that humanism turns itself into a kind of patent antihumanism? Or does the end of humanism open another meaning in which the classic figure of *humanitas* lends itself to new interpretive possibilities? We must begin by saying no to nostalgia for and restoration of *humanitas* like the one that Lukács called for at the end of the war against the alleged destroyers of reason; or today, certainly in more sophisticated fashion, like the one that Habermas implicitly proposed. As the German philosopher Peter Sloterdijk has argued, against Habermas, both the humanism of the first modern age and its political retranslation in the national cultures of the nineteenth century are fundamentally exhausted.[11] Contemporary societies no longer produce their political syntheses according to the model of literary society. Nor, moreover, would it have been imaginable, after the end of the Hitler youth, to reanimate a new Goethean youth. Heidegger himself did not address his "Letter" to the German nation, as Fichte did in his day, but to a foreign correspondent: the Frenchman Jean Beaufret. We might say, if we want to continue to employ the term, that today *humanitas* can no longer be understood in a national-traditional key but in a different and larger sense that I would call both singular and global. *Humanitas* ought to refer to each man and to the entire world. Thus, regardless of its contradictions and the instrumental use that has been made of it, Nietzsche's thought signals a threshold of awareness behind which we can no longer retreat. Unlike what all preceding essentialisms, historicisms, or lay or religious personalisms propose or presuppose, man's humanity can no longer be thought outside the concept, or, better, the natural reality, of *bíos*. Singular and collective life, in its demands for conservation and development, is the only criterion today for universal legitimization that anchors the political, social, and cultural practices of our world. This means that the notion of human nature, which is more and more central to both scientific and philosophical work, must be thought not in opposition to, but in relation with the notion of history.

In this sense, Darwin's first intuition, not only that shouldn't we exclude invariance and mutation but that they co-implicate each other, must once again be considered seriously (naturally, with all necessary modifications). In the human being, it is an innate endowment that opens up a range of possibilities for acquisition that, in time, are reflected retroactively in the genetic code itself. Man, we might say, is programmed to continually change his programming. Philosopher and medical historian Georges Canguilhem was able to argue that, for a human being, rather than being a state of static normality, health actually consists of the capacity for an organism to continually modify its own norms. Conversely, sickness is nothing but the atrophy, or the weakening of this innovative potential.[12] Basically, Canguilhem's is a new way of understanding Pico's concept of the infinite variety of human nature by transporting it within the body. Such variety, rather than being thought of as the miraculous removal of the laws of biology, should instead be thought of expressly as the specific effect of those laws. If this is true, Cartesian metaphysical dualism and biosociological reductionism turn out to be two opposing and complementary sides of the same error that would consist in the first instance of absorbing the invariant within the contingent and, in the other, dissolving the contingent into the invariant. Rather, the topical locus of philosophical and scientific inquiry is situated precisely at the junction, or in the zone of indistinction, between natural regularities and historicocultural variations.[13] It makes little sense to say that this renders the opposition between sciences of the spirit and the natural sciences, and between the empirical and the transcendental, entirely obsolete (and therefore deeply conservative). Just as the activities of the mind and language are connected to the organic structures that innervate them, so are they over time modified by the linguistic and mental performance that they produce. If, for example, the movement of the hand depends on the brain's command, so the functioning of the brain is dependent on the operations of the hand. In this sense, it's clear that the entire course of history is the free and infinitely variable effect of a bionatural necessity.

If this is true, so too the inverse: Just as nature strongly influences history, so history reacts in an equally significant way on nature. And here we come to the most complex and problematic aspect of the question, which we might call, after and together with the "Darwin side," the "Nietzsche side." It consists of what we defined earlier as the anthrotechnological, or anthropoietic vector, that is increasingly at work in the contemporary world. Let's say that in Nietzsche's time, as well as during the mad Nazi biocracy, the possibilities for artificially modifying human nature opened up considerably. I'm not thinking only about technobiologies but, more generally, about the drastic decline in mediations between the spheres of politics, law, and economy on the one side, and the dimension of *bíos* on the other.

When one quite correctly speaks of biopolitics, one refers to the fact that the faculties that define man historically, as well as those that define him with regard to his nature, are heavily invested by sociopolitical processes. This is the only way to explain otherwise undecipherable phenomena such as, on the one hand, the new weight ethnicity has in contemporary political conflict and, on the other, the productive use in the working world of an eminently natural faculty such as that of linguistic communication. Despite the profound differences between these two phenomena, what occurs in both is the inscription of practices of political power [*potere*] and economic production within the sphere of *bíos*. Or, seen differently: the powerful entry of biological life into sociopolitical practices. When you add to such processes the expansion of real and true biotechnology (which is authorized by the hyperdevelopment of genetic and cognitive engineering), the picture that emerges appears troubling, to say the least. By now, even with regard to Foucault's classic analyses of the disciplinary control of bodies by certain political regimes, we find ourselves today facing a much riskier situation in which the very subject of biopower tends to widen and to become generalized in planetary *dispositifs* that regulate life according to entirely technicalized procedures.

Still, regardless of the inherent risks of such transformations, they should not be understood only for their terrifying effect, as in the posthumous triumph of the inhuman prognosticated by "bio-catastrophists."[14] And here's why: because technology is not necessarily in opposition to nature (indeed, in some ways it springs forth from it), insofar as human nature presents an originary technicalness, as every individual movement of our body and every sound of our voice is technical. Furthermore, every use of technology, from the most simple to the most sophisticated, influences our nature. If we measure technology on a phylogenetic level, every technology is in principle biotechnology. Thus certainly technology is not merely the production of manufactured goods but also a transformation of the one who produces them, an alteration not only of material and environment but also of man. And this is the most delicate point, on the basis of which the entire discourse on humanism might acquire a different and unexpected meaning. The fact is, humanisms, even classical humanisms, are not all the same. Writing against the anthropocentric essentialism of those who saw in man an absolute and unique model, authors like Bruno and Spinoza give us a sense of the absolute multiplicity of forms that human nature can assume. Diversity, alterity, hybridization are not necessarily limits or dangers against which one must be on guard in the name of the self-centered pureness of the individual and the species—this according to an immunitary semantics that led to some of the most brutal forms of homicidal eugenics. If we move these concepts out from within the exclusive logic of *immunitas* to the open and inclusive one of *communitas*, they can actually be considered a richness and an opportunity.[15] The two should not be separated, in the sense that the infraspecific relationship between man and animal, which dates back to the age of domestication, constituted the first anthropotechnical, and therefore self-transformative, segment in the entire process of homination. This is why—contrary to what is accepted by the beastialization of the enemy, which all ancient and recent racisms engaged in the symbolic fabrication of the man-animal employ deliberately—the relationship, even the conjugation with the theriosphere (or the animal world), has always constituted a decisive advancement of human culture.[16] Unlike in Heidegger's thought, the animal is not the ancestral past, the stone face, or the mute enigma but the future of man: a place and a threshold from which man can draw stimuli for a more complex and open elaboration of his own *humanitas*. One could say something analogous about technology, insofar as it doesn't patently contradict the biological possibilities contained within our naturally altered nature but instead carries them to their maximum development. Clearly, like every opportunity for conclusion, so is this one found on the other side of a considerable risk. On the two folds of this page, the history and the destiny of what comes after humanism is written in letters not yet entirely legible.

TOTALITARIANISM OR BIOPOLITICS: TOWARD A PHILOSOPHICAL INTERPRETATION OF THE TWENTIETH CENTURY

Toward a philosophical interpretation of the twentieth century. How should we understand this expression? What meaning should we assign it? We might suggest two different answers to these questions, which are in some ways even contradictory. The first is the classic answer, associated with the great twentieth-century philosophical tradition of Husserl, Heidegger, and Sartre, to mention a few of the most well-known names. This answer calls for a reading of contemporary historical events through an interpretative lens that philosophy itself provides and singles out as the only one capable of grasping its essence. Whether such an interpretive lens is identified as the crisis of European science, the deployment of nihilism, or the liberation of oppressed peoples (in line with the thinkers mentioned above), the twentieth century is interpreted according to the internal demands of a given philosophy that is charged with providing the period meaning. According to this model, twentieth-century phenomena are located along a single trajectory. History and philosophy are therefore categorically distinct fields, and only philosophy is assigned the task of granting total meaning to a series of otherwise senseless facts.

To this first answer (which did, however, give rise to analyses of great importance), we may juxtapose another—one that's bound to overturn the logic of the first. This second answer reconfigures the relationship between philosophy and history; it no longer aims to subordinate historical dynamics to the logic of a given philosophy but aims instead to grasp an element or a characteristic that is itself philosophical within certain historical events. In this case, meaning is no longer impressed upon historical events from the outside, from a philosophical perspective that contemplates them, but as something that originates from and is made up of the facts themselves—that is, their novelty, significance, and effects. Perhaps this shift in viewpoint resounds in what great twentieth-century philosophy, from Heidegger to Wittgenstein and Kojève, defined on the one hand as the "end of philosophy" and on the other as the "end of history." In reality, what was ending was a way of looking at history as the object of philosophical practice. Thenceforth, we might say, history was no longer the object but, if anything, the subject of philosophy, just as philosophy became no longer the form but the content of history. Because if the events of our time are loaded with philosophical weight, then the task of reflection will no longer be to attribute history a suitable meaning for such events but instead to confront the original meaning of the events themselves. Still, we ought to bear in mind that history does not contain a single, presupposed meaning (which was the pretense of all philosophies of history, whether progressive or regressive, ascending or descending); instead, it is constituted by a comparison and a confrontation between multiple vectors of meaning which are often in competition among themselves. The events that are the most laden with meaning, for example, the attack on the Twin Towers in 2001, are the very ones that determine an unexpected overturning of all previous meaning and suddenly open a new and different source of signification. It is in this radical way that we should understand the expression that contemporary history is eminently philosophical. This is not to say that history can only be understood from the viewpoint of philosophy, and much less from the even more reductive points of view such as economy or sociology, or even political science (as Augusto Del Noce precociously argued upon deaf ears)[1] but instead that history's decisive events—namely world wars, the advent of technology, globalization, terrorism—are philosophical powers [*potenze*] that struggle to take over the world and dominate our interpretation of it, and thus its ultimate meaning. For this reason, more than oil, arms or democracy, the metaphysical stakes of the conflict underway lie in the definition of the meaning of contemporary history.

I'd like to relate these two ways of understanding contemporary history—that is, a philosophy *of* history and history *as* philosophy—to two hermeneutic paradigms that are often confused and superimposed upon one another, despite the fact that they are radically different in both their presuppositions and effects. I'm referring to the paradigms of totalitarianism and biopolitics. Despite attempts to hold them together in a single frame that makes one the continuation and confirmation of the other, in terms of either a biopolitical totalitarianism or a totalitarian biopolitics, we're actually dealing with two interpretative models that not only are logically divergent but are actually bound to exclude one another reciprocally. At the heart of their divergence lies a difference not so much in content but in form. Totalitarianism and biopolitics differ first and foremost on how they formulate the relationship between philosophy and history, and the way they consider how history is thought *by* and *in* philosophy.

According to the model of totalitarianism, history is read along a continuum of chronological succession. History is split by a fundamental fracture between two choices—namely, democracy or totalitarianism—which succeed one another and alternate throughout time. In the middle decades of the twentieth century, a long phase characterized by the comprehensive development of liberal democracy is followed by a season of totalitarianism in both the West and East. This phase is, in turn, eclipsed by the renewed victory of the now hegemonic liberal-democratic model of the West, once in 1945, and again in 1989. This produces a double historical-philosophical configuration, wherein modern history is situated along a single vertical line. At first, this line is ascendant and progressive; then, beginning in the 1920s, it is regressive and degrading. Finally, in the second half of the twentieth century, it is turned once again in the proper direction (despite the risks of decline that are taking shape today, above all in the Islamic world). Corresponding to these fractures along the vertical axis, there is a horizontal axis that hosts a substantial homogeneity of forms, contents, and languages (however profoundly different they may seem from one another). Here I refer not only to Nazism and communism, which are superimposed on one another to form a single conceptual block, but also to liberalism and democracy, which are superimposed on one another without much difficulty by a philosophy of history that is more inclined to assimilate than to differentiate. The totalitarian paradigm's repeated and contradictory recourse to the category of the "origin" only confirms the fact that totalitarianism makes use of a rather traditional philosophy of history. That the term *origin* appears in two of its most significant texts, namely Arendt's *The Origins of Totalitarianism* and Talmon's *The Origins of Totalitarian Democracy*, is no mere coincidence but instead a clear sign of how a category that is supposedly new (totalitarianism) inheres within a philosophical frame that is absolutely classical.[2] In all of the philosophical work on totalitarianism, the interpreter directs his or her gaze at the origin. This research is preoccupied with such questions as: Whence was it born? What created it? What is the primary foundation of what twentieth-century totalitarianism brings into the world? But it is precisely here, in this question about origins, that the principal antinomy of the entire paradigm becomes clear: How do we trace the genesis of a totalitarian phenomenon that also declares itself to be inassimilable to every other of government, and therefore far removed from every genetic sequence of causality? Why look for the origin of something that seems not to have one? How to hold together the discontinuity of principle—the absolute *novum* of the totalitarian event, and the continuity of fact—its derivation from an origin that precedes it?

There are two possible strategies for answering this question, both of which are typical of the historicist model. The first approach, which Arendt takes up, traces the entire western political tradition back to an originary loss (of the Greek *polis*), which condemns all subsequent history to a depoliticization that is destined to flow into the antipolitical drift of totalitarian domination. Twentieth-century totalitarianism, understood as a dynamic, or indeed a logic which is itself unitary, thus ends up appearing as the necessary outcome of an equally homogenous logic, such as the one that undergirds modernity as a whole. It is indeed true that, again according to Arendt, between modernity and totalitarianism a sudden acceleration occurs that differentiates among their features, though they both run along the same line of development that begins with Hobbes (interpreted clumsily as the one who "provided political thought with the prerequisite for all race doctrines")[3] and precipitates into the abyss of Auschwitz and Kolyma.

The other road, taken first by Talmon and then quite differently by François Furet, is one that searches for the origin of totalitarianism within the very democratic tradition to which it should set itself in opposition.[4] Again, in this case, the meaning of totalitarianism is identified as an originary sickness that is situated, if no longer in Hobbes or Rousseau, in the most decisive and suggestive event of modernity: the French Revolution.

Yet in this way totalitarianism remains encaged in another antinomy that is just as relevant as the first: If the reference to the French Revolution (that is, to the experiment of a most radical political democratization) makes sense in terms of communism, how then do we also explain Nazism through it?

This is a difficulty, a logical gap that not even Arendt's great essay managed to avoid, split in two, as it was from its initial drafting, between a masterful genealogical reconstruction of Nazi anti-Semitism dating back to the war years and a subsequent and overlapping (if weaker) section comparing it with Stalinist communism, which was clearly conditioned by the climate of an incipient Cold War. The reason for this unevenness, which we can trace empirically to the closure of the Soviet archives, is to be found at a critical point in the interpretative model she deploys—that is, in the difficulty of locating the roots of Soviet communism in the same degenerative drift, namely, from the crisis of the nation-state to colonial imperialism and the explosion of biological racism—that brought us to Nazism. How does one hold together, in a single categorical horizon, a hypernaturalistic conception, such as that of the Nazis, with the historicist paroxysm of communism? What does a theory of absolute equality, philosophically speaking, have to do with a theory, and a practice, of absolute difference such as Nazism? A drawing of two solid colors, composed of a single, vertical opposition between the time for democracy and the time for totalitarianism, seems to take shape behind the enormous logical, categorical, and linguistic caesurae that cut modern history with a complexity that cannot be contained by the mesh grating that encloses the totalitarian paradigm.

It's no coincidence that, precisely because of this logical and historical difficulty, while Arendt's remains a great book on Nazism, the subsequent ones by Aron, Tamlon, and Furet are books about communism and only it. In his essay on *Democracy and Totalitarianism*, Aron explains the motivation for his choice (which is actually a necessity) of communist totalitarianism over the Nazi variant by suggesting that what interests him are regimes that don't simply declare themselves democratic but instead are actually derived from a perverse deviation from democracy.[5] Both Talmon and Furet, but also Gauchet and Lefort, validate Aron's thesis: Totalitarianism, naturally that of a leftist stripe, is born from the ailing rib of democracy, and not outside of it.[6] Actually, the totalitarian regime arises not from a defect in but, if anything, from an excess or a surplus of democracy—a democracy that is as radical, extreme, and absolute as it is full of egalitarian substance, so much that it shatters its own formal limits and implodes into its opposite. Communism, according to Gauchet's thesis, is instituted through a perverse overturning of the democratic model that fancifully distorts democracy's characteristics without altering its presupposition. Communism is both the dream and the nightmare of democracy. At this point, we can begin to make out the chain of aporias that characterize the totalitarian paradigm. If communism is not merely situated within the conceptual horizon of democracy that sprung forth from the French Revolution but in a certain sense carries it to completion and, in so doing, to dissolution—if communism is bound to democracy in its genesis and its egalitarian excess, how can we still maintain a fundamental distinction between totalitarianism and democracy? How can totalitarianism define itself in opposition to what germinates it? Secondly, if such an antonymic link with democracy exists for communism, this is certainly not true for Nazism, which is consistently removed from the analytical frame by these writers. But in this case, the very logical consistency of the category of totalitarianism fails. While the category of totalitarianism was already wobbly at the historical level, it also crumbles on the philosophical one, the very level that was supposed to provide it stability.

Unlike the totalitarian paradigm, biopolitics is based neither upon a philosophical presupposition nor upon a philosophy of history but upon concrete events. Moreover, it is based not solely on facts but on the effective languages that render these facts intelligible. Even before Foucault's analysis, we ought to turn to Nietzsche's genealogy, and more precisely to his deconstruction of the concept of origin (an origin which is still sought after by theorists of totalitarianism), in order to identify the perspective of this new gaze.[7] If a full and absolute origin of historical process does not exist, if the origin is never singular, if it is doubled or multiplied into so many origins that they are no longer definable as such (as Nietzsche explains in radical contrast to all philosophical historicism), then the entire historical course of the West is destined to assume characteristics that may not be reduced to the linearity of such a perspective.[8] This profoundly alters our entire interpretation of modernity. As a consequence, any possibility of a comprehensive reading of modernity gives way to a frame that is cut through by horizontal and vertical gaps that break any presumption of continuity. Moreover, what in the totalitarian paradigm was configured as a series of events that were entirely contained within a specialized political language is now widened to a more complex relationship that stems from the encounter or confrontation with, or the superimposition of, other disciplinary vocabularies that interact with and contaminate one another with unprecedented effects. Rather than predisposing the entire frame of modern philosophy toward a single depoliticizing drift (as in Arendt's model), the entry of biological life onto the scene upsets it, plotting it out along different vectors of sense that overlap or conflict without ever merging completely into a single flow. The strength of the biopolitical perspective resides precisely in its capacity to read this interweaving and conflict, this gap and implication, or the powerfully antinomic outcome of the intersection between originally heterogeneous languages, such as those of politics and biology. What occurs when an "outside"—namely, life—bursts into the sphere of politics, causing its supposed autonomy to explode and shifting the discourse to a terrain that is irreducible to the traditional terms (such as democracy, power [*potere*], and ideology) of modern political philosophy?

It's in this frame that we should situate the phenomenon of Nazism and interrogate its radical heterogeneity. Without even considering the most recent interpretations, a witness such as Ernst Nolte (whom we could not accuse of exhibiting pro-Gauchet sympathies) identified the theoretical fallacy of situating an ideology like that of communism, however catastrophic in its political consequences, on the same plane as Nazism, which could in no way belong to the same category.[9] For Nolte, unlike Arendt, Nazism is not an "ideology," because it belongs to a realm that is both below and different from that of "ideas," from which Marxist communism is born. Nazism is not a different species within the same totalitarian genus, because it is situated outside that Western tradition that also counts among its most farthest-flung offspring the philosophy of communism. In contrast to the Western philosophical tradition, which despite its internal differences is unified by a common reference to a universal, transcendent type, Nazism elaborates a radically different conception that no longer needs to legitimate itself in an idea, whatever it may be, because it finds its crucial foundation in its basic material strength. This, in turn, is not the necessary and contingent product of a history that defines the relationship between men on the basis of their free decisions, or even, as communism claims, based on their social conditions, but instead based on an absolutely natural given that concerns the bare [*nuda*] biological sphere. Recognizing within Nazism the unprecedented attempt to liberate the natural features of existence from their historical distinctiveness means overturning the Arendtian thesis about the totalitarian superimposition of the philosophy of nature and the philosophy of history; it means identifying the blind spot within the inability of nature and history to be absorbed within one another and therefore the philosophical impracticability of the notion of totalitarianism.

When considered from a biopolitical point of view, the twentieth century, and indeed the entire course of modernity, is determined or decided not by the superficial and contradictory antithesis between totalitarianism and democracy but instead by the much deeper antithesis (because it has to do with the preservation of life) between history and nature, between the historicization of nature and the naturalization of history. In addition, this opposition is much deeper because it may not be ascribed to a symmetrical bipolarity, because nature (understood in the biological sense, as Nazism did) is not antihistory, or a philosophy or ideology that opposes history, but a non-philosophy and a non-ideology. It is not a political philosophy but a biological politics, a politics of life and on life that is turned into its opposite and thus productive of death. As Levinas wrote as early as the 1930s, in Nazism, "the biological, with all the fatality that it entails, becomes more than an *object* of spiritual life; it becomes its heart."[10] It is this immediately bio- and therefore thanatopolitical element of Nazism, and not the number of its victims (which was even less than those claimed by Stalinist communism), that rendered the category of totalitarianism historically and theoretically useless.

Contrary to the illusions of those who imagined that the double catastrophe, one by explosion and the other by implosion, of what were called totalitarianisms would allow us to return to the old political lexicon that preceded them, the question of biopolitics remains with us ever more. From this point of view, the end of the Second World War does not signal, either at the level of language or at the level of material practice, the victory of the alliance between democracy and communism but the victory of a liberalism that is situated within the very biopolitical regime that, though configured in the opposite way, gave rise to Nazism. I would add that, in this way, Nazism is much more contemporary [*nuovo*] than communism insofar as it emerges from the war definitively defeated at the military and political level, but not entirely so at the cultural and linguistic one; the centrality of *bios* as the object and subject of politics is confirmed, even if it is altered in a liberal key as the appropriation, and possible modification, of the body on the part not of the state but of the individual who is owner [*proprietario*] of himself. If for Nazism man *is* his own body and only this, for liberalism beginning with Locke, man *has*, or possesses, his own body, and therefore he can use, transform, and sell it as an inner slave. In this sense, liberalism (naturally I'm talking about conceptual categories) overturns the Nazi perspective, transferring the ownership of the body from the state to the individual, but within the same biopolitical lexicon. It is this biopolitical characterization of liberalism that separates it from democracy. To hazard a not entirely unjustified exaggeration, we might say that, after all of the so-called totalitarianisms, the reason it is not possible to return to liberal democracy lies in the fact that liberal democracy has never existed as such. Just as we should deconstruct the absorption of Nazism and communism within the category of totalitarianism, it is equally clear that we ought to problematize the notion of liberal democracy. As Carl Schmitt pointed out in an important 1920s essay on the parliamentary system and democracy, the ideology of liberalism is quite different from, if not opposed to, the universalistic and egalitarian ideology of democracy because its logic, pre-suppositions, and conceptual language are anti-egalitarian, particularistic, and at times even naturalistic.[11] If we think of modernity not in historical terms, that is, if we reject the notion of a chronological succession between liberal-democratic and totalitarian regimes, but instead in genealogical or topological terms, we see that the real fault line, the conceptually significant distinction, is not the vertical one between totalitarianism and liberal democracy but the horizontal one that cuts across democracy and communism on the one side (communism being the paroxysmal completion of egalitarian democracy) and biopolitics on the other, which itself is split into two antithetical forms that are not unrelated: Nazism and liberalism, or State biopolitics and individual biopolitics.

Moreover, Foucault himself identified the biopolitical character of liberalism by situating it at the level of government of life and therefore opposed, or at least extraneous to, the universalistic procedures of democracy.[12] Democracy that is founded on the primacy of abstract law and the equal rights of individuals who possess reason and will ended in the 1920s and 1930s and is no longer able to be rebuilt, much less exported elsewhere. Naturally, if we reduce the democratic regime to the mere presence of multiple parties that are formally in competition and of the electoral system which forms governmental majorities, we can always claim, as some have recently, that the number of democracies in the world continues to grow. Still, if we look at it this way, we lose sight of the radical transformation that the concept of democracy presupposes. Let me be clear: In maintaining such a thesis, I'm not referring to those dysfunctions, defects, limits, or contradictions that are implicit in every political form, which are instead necessarily imperfect and incomplete. I refer instead to a deep laceration within the democratic horizon itself, which comes into view as soon as we shift our gaze from the plane of form to that of content, to the "material" of the current political regime. It's true that democracy as such does not have "content"; it is a technology [*tecnica*], an ensemble of rules designed to distribute power [*potere*] in a way that is proportionate to the will of the electorate. But it's for this very reason that it explodes, or implodes, as soon as it is filled up with a substance that it cannot contain without changing into something radically different.

That substance is precisely the biological life of individuals and of the population that installs itself at the center of all significant political decisions. Naturally, this doesn't mean that in the encounter and confrontation between political forces other choices that have to do with international relations and domestic order, models of economic development, and definitions of civil rights are not also in play. But the explosive element with regard to the traditional democratic framework lies in the fact that every one of these choices refers directly to the body of its citizens. If we consider that, in Italy, for example, the laws that have engaged public opinion the most were those on the smoking ban, drugs, public safety, immigration, and artificial insemination, we can grasp the measure and the direction of this paradigm shift: The model of the medical cure has become not only the privileged object but the very form of political life—and therefore of a politics that finds only in life the sole source of possible legitimation. This is what happens when citizens are repeatedly interpellated by, or in any case objectively involved in, questions related to the conservation, the borders, or the exclusion of their own bodies. But, and here we arrive at the decisive point, the moment in which the living, or dying, body becomes the symbolic and material epicenter of political dynamics and battles, we enter a realm that is not simply, as some say, "after" or "beyond" but decidedly outside of democracy.[13] Not only outside of its procedures, but outside of its language, its conceptual framework. Democracy always addresses a group of subjects who are made equal precisely because they are separated from their own bodies insofar as they are understood as pure logical atoms endowed with rational wills. Even this element of abstraction, of disembodiment, resounds in the proposition that places the person at the center of democratic practice, wherein for "person" is meant (according the original meaning of the term) precisely a disincarnated subjectivity that is, if you will, distinguished from that ensemble of impulses, needs, and desires that are bound up in the corporeal dimension.[14] When, with the biopolitical turn that we are reconstructing, this very corporeal dimension becomes the true interlocutor—the subject and object of government—the principle of equality above all else is up for discussion, insofar as it is inapplicable to something (such as the body) that is constitutively different from all others according to criteria that are at times determinable and alterable. But not only is the principle of equality up for debate; so is a whole spate of distinctions, or oppositions, on which—before democracy itself—the entire conception of modern politics from which it is born rests—that is, between public and private, artificial and natural, law and theology. Because as soon as the body substitutes, or "fills in," the abstract subjectivity of the juridical person, it is difficult, if not impossible, to distinguish what concerns the public sphere from what concerns the private one. But, in addition, it is difficult to distinguish what belongs to the natural order and what may be submitted to technological intervention, with all of the ethical and religious questions that such a choice carries with it.

The reason for such an indistinction, and for the unruly contrasts that it inevitably causes, is that human life is precisely where public and private, natural and artificial, political and theological interweave to form a bind that no majority decision is capable of dissolving. This is why its centrality is incompatible with the conceptual lexicon of democracy. Contrary to what one might imagine, the emergence of life within the apparatuses [*dispositivi*] of power [*potere*] signals the eclipse of democracy, at least of the kind of democracy that we have imagined up to this point. Naturally, this doesn't mean that another kind of democracy is impossible, one that is compatible with the biopolitical turn that is in progress and at this point irreversible. But where to look for, how to think, what a biopolitical democracy, or a democratic biopolitics, that is capable of exercising itself not on bodies but in favor of them might mean today is quite difficult to identify conclusively. At the moment we can only glimpse it. What is certain is that to think in this direction we would need to divest ourselves of all the old philosophies of history and all of the conceptual paradigms to which they refer.

TOWARD A PHILOSOPHY OF THE IMPERSONAL

Never before has the notion of the person constituted such an indispensable point of reference for all philosophical, political, and juridical discourses that lay claim to the value of human life as such. Setting aside ideological and theoretical differences, not one of them casts doubt on the importance of the category of the person, which is the indisputable (and undisputed) premise of each perspective. This tacit convergence is especially evident in the contentious field of bioethics. Actually, though, the clash (however bitter) between secularists and Catholics hinges upon the precise moment in which a living being can be considered a person (at conception for Catholics, later for secularists), but not on the decisive value in attributing personhood to a living being. Whether one becomes a person by divine decree or through nature, this is the threshold, the crucial passage through which meaningless biological matter becomes something intangible. What is presumed here, more than other criteria or normative principles, is the absolute ontological prevalence, the incommensurable surplus, of what is personal with regard to what is not. Only a life that has passed through that symbolic door capable of endowing the credentials of the person may be considered sacred or of qualitative value.

At the level of law, we find the same presupposition but now reinforced by even more elaborate arguments. In order to claim what we call subjective rights, we must enter, at least in the modern juridical conception, the circumscribed space of the person, just as being a person means to enjoy such rights for oneself. The most frequently heard thesis (here I refer to work being done in Italy by Stefano Rodotà and Luigi Ferrajoli) is that the increasing value of the category of the person lies in the fact that only it is capable of filling the gap that the modern State initially established between the concepts of man and citizen.[1] As Hannah Arendt argued just after the Second World War, this gap grew from the underlying local character of the category of the citizen, understood as a member of a given national community and therefore incapable of being extended to every one. Only a potentially universal notion like that of the person, it was believed, would have permitted extending fundamental rights to every human being. At this point, as Martha Nussbaum argued in a recent book, there was a widespread cultural call to shift from the restricted notion of the citizen, or even the individual, to the more general one of the person.[2]

The same ideas circulated within theoretical research. Reflections on personal identity, and with it a renewed interest in the category of the person, constitute one of the rare intersections between Anglo-Saxon analytic philosophy and so-called continental philosophy. Naturally, they employ different categories, but they operate within the same horizon of meaning, which contains a privileged reference to the notion of the person. If analytic philosophers, from Strawson to Parfit, consider the person to be the crucial starting point for the elaboration of a complete ontology of subjectivity, Italian philosophers writing from a phenomenological perspective have argued for a new philosophy of the person, based on a renewed interest in the personalistic phenomenology of Edith Stein.[3] All this while, years ago, Paul Ricoeur took up and launched again Catholic French Personalism in a hermeneutic key. If in contemporary culture an uncontestable point of convergence, almost a postulate that legitimizes every "philosophically correct" discourse, is to be found, it is the affirmation of the person and the philosophical, religious, ethical, and political value in doing so. No other concept in the Western tradition seems to enjoy the same general and crosscutting consensus. Moreover, the Universal Declaration of Human Rights of 1948 took the notion of person as its basis: After the catastrophe of war and the defeat of an idea, such as that of the Nazis (which aimed directly at flattening human identity to bare biology), it seemed that only the idea of the person could reconstruct the broken link between man and citizen, body and soul, rights and life. And just as today's globalization is shattering the old world order, philosophical, juridical, and political thought turns with even greater conviction than before, entrusting itself to the unifying value of the category of the person.

With what result? Even a cursory glance at the international scene raises troubling questions about how human rights, beginning with the first one, the right to life, and in ways never before, have been profoundly negated. No right appears more swept aside by the millions suffering from hunger, sickness, and war than the right to life. How is this possible and where does the drift to negating life originate, especially now when all languages uphold the normative reference to the value of the person? We might respond, as some often do, that this happens because we haven't fully taken up the person, that the reference to it is still in some way partial, that it's been rolled back, or that it's incomplete. Frankly, the reply seems both historically and conceptually weak. My impression, which I've set out more fully in a recent book, is that thought has headed in a symmetrically opposite direction: It is a question not of the restricted, partial, or incomplete extension of the ideology of the person but instead of the invasiveness of the ideology of the person, an excess that produces these kinds of counterfactual outcomes. If the fog hiding a central principle that looks more and more like a true personalist fundamentalism were to lift, we would see that the category of the person cannot heal or fill the gap between rights and man, which would make something like human rights possible, because it's precisely the category of person that produces and widens the gap between rights and man to begin with. The problem we face—that is, the absolute impracticability of the rights of man as such—arises not because we haven't completely moved into the regime of the person but rather because that we haven't yet left it behind.

I realize I'm claiming something, a line of reasoning, that contradicts a solid body of evidence within the modern tradition, or that is even constitutive of modernity itself.[4] But I believe we have to take a long look back in order to see, behind and within, the obvious epochal discontinuities, the underlying nodes, and profound articulations that are less evident but just as operative. From this point of view, operating both vertically and horizontally, the person appears to be more than just a concept but a truly long-standing performative *dispositif*, whose first output was to erase its own genealogy and, along with it, its real effects. Such a genealogy of the person ought to be reconstructed in all its complexity, beginning with the initial distinction, but also the relation, between its Christian and Roman roots—

because it's precisely at their point of intersection that we can identify that capacity [*potenza*] for separation and selection that forms the most important effect of the apparatus of the person itself. An element of doubling is already implicit in the idea of the mask, whose etymology is found in the Greek *prosopon* and in the Latin *persona*. Though the mask sticks, or is "glued" to the face of the actor playing the character, the face never becomes one with the mask. Not even in the case of the ritual of burial masks, where the real spiritual nature of the man that it covers is supposed to shine through, does this difference fail to appear. On the contrary, in this case the originary schism (dear to the Christian tradition) is emphasized, according to which the separation between the person and the living body that holds the mask grants entry into the afterlife. Both the idea of the double nature of Christ and that of the Trinity confirm this inner gap, this structural doubling of the personal dimension: The unity between human and divine nature, or between body and soul, must always endure an indelible separation within the person.

In the Roman concept of the person one finds an even more pronounced separation, insofar as it is codified according to a doctrinal apparatus. Despite all of the changes across the different phases of Roman law, what doesn't change is the principal difference between the artificial person and man as a living being in whom the former inheres.[5] The clearest testament to such a separating *dispositif* lies in the fact that, as is well known, not all men in Rome were able to be defined as men in every respect. The *patres* (free, adult males) are distinguished from the slaves, who in Roman law are categorized as things, or else they are situated somewhere between thing and person. Without lingering over the multiple typologies of men that the Roman juridical machine anticipates, or, better still, produces, what counts for our discussion is the effect of de-personalization (the reduction to the status of thing) that is implicit in the concept of the person: The very definition of the person is born negatively from its presumed difference from men and women who are not persons, or who are only partially and temporarily persons and as such always at risk of falling into the status of thing. What Roman law achieves with such incomparable categorical imagination is not only the distinction among persons, semipersons, and nonpersons but also elaborations of intermediate situations, zones of indistinction, and exceptions that regulate the movement, or the oscillation, from one status to another. That every son was, at least in ancient times, subject to the power of life and death by his father, who was authorized to kill, sell, loan, or abandon him, means that in Rome no one, even if born free, is guaranteed the status of the person. Being a person is anything but a natural given—it is the artificial protrusion, the exceptional residue that is distinguished from a common servile condition. No one is born a person. One can become one, but only by pushing others into the realm of the thing.

This procedure of selection and exclusion through the *dispositif* of the person that is typical of Roman law spreads, albeit transformed, to modern juridical systems—as historians of law who have been able to make out the lines of continuity that determine even the most radical changes have shown. Now, without diminishing the epochal difference between the objectivistic conception of Roman law and the individualistic subjectivism of modern law, the trait that binds them within the same semantic orbit can be found in the presumed difference between the status of the person and the body of the human being into which it is implanted. Only a nonperson, or a living material that is not personal, can give rise to something like a person as the background and the object of another's sovereignty. Over time, however, the person is such only if he or she reduces a part, or the whole, of his or her body to the thing. Not only does *persona* not coincide with *homo* (which in Latin is used to identify primarily slaves) but *persona* is defined by its difference from *homo*. Embedded in our contemporary moment like an archaic nucleus, this is fundamentally why the category of the person blocks us from thinking a properly human right and actually renders such a right conceptually impossible. *Person* is the technical term that separates juridical capacity from the naturalness of being human, and thus it distinguishes each person from his or her own way of being. It is the noncoincidence, or even divergence, of men and women from their respective ways of being.

When Hobbes argues afterward that "a person is he whose words or actions are considered either as his own, or as representing the words or actions of another man," he merely completes a schism, with the result that the term *person* can be used for a nonhuman entity such as a church, a hospital, or a bridge.[6] The mask not only fails to stick to the face it covers but can actually cover, as in represent, the face of another. While it is true that, beginning with the French Revolution, all men were declared equal insofar as they were subjected equally to the law, the fact remains that this attribution of subjectivity refers to a noncorporeal, or more-than-corporeal element that inhabits the body, and which divides it into two parts: one rational, spiritual, or moral (which is the personal), and the other animal. It's no accident that, at the very moment that the Declaration of Human Rights of 1948 was being formulated, Catholic philosopher Jacques Maritain could argue that the term *person* refers to one who is capable of exercising mastery over his biological and properly animal part. "If a sound political conception," he writes, "depends above all upon concentrating on the human person, it must at the same time bear in mind the fact that this person is that of animal gifted with reason, and that the part of animality in such a set-up is immense."[7] From here, we have a double separation. The first is within one man, divided between a personal and an animal life. The second is between men who are persons (insofar as they are capable of dominating the irrational part of themselves) and men who are incapable of such self-rule and thus situated at a level below that of the person. We are dealing with a logical construct that nevertheless produces powerful effects on our categories of thought and which date back to the beginning of our philosophical tradition. As Heidegger sensed, as soon as man is defined as a "rational animal" (according to the Aristotelian formulation from which Maritain draws), one has to opt for one of two possibilities, which ultimately mirror one another: Either reduce rational man to corporeal man (as Nazism did) or, conversely, subject the former to domination by the latter (as the Personalist tradition has always done).

The *dispositif* that separates and excludes, that crosses and moves beyond the conventional opposition between secular and Catholic culture, finds its fullest expression in liberal bioethics—precisely because the origin of the distinction between the two cultures lies in a concept (that of the person) that, from its inception, has a double connotation that is both Catholic and Roman, both theological and juridical. Whereas for Locke and Mill a person is only one who is proprietor of his own body, writers such as Hugo Engelhardt and Peter Singer take up the Roman doctrine that initially distinguishes between person and non-person, through the intermediate stages of the almost-person, the semi-person, and the temporary person. Furthermore, they assign to true and proper persons the power to keep the less-than-proper person alive or to push them toward death depending upon the needs of the social and economic order. As if further proof were needed, consider the structural connection between movements of personalization and depersonalization that only appear to be at odds. Every attribution of personality always implicitly contains a reification of the impersonal biological layer from which attributing personality distances itself. Only when human beings are assimilable to things do others have to be defined as persons. In order for some to be labeled persons, a feature is needed that differentiates them from those who are no longer persons, not yet persons, or not persons in any way. The *dispositif* of the person thus both superimposes and juxtaposes humans as men and animals as men, or distinguishes a truly human part of man from another, beastly character who is his slave. Yet in separating life from itself, the *dispositif* of the person is also the conceptual instrument through which some part of the person may be killed. The liberal Peter Singer argues, "At present parents can choose to keep or destroy their disabled offspring only if the disability happens to be detected during pregnancy. There is no logical basis for restricting parents' choice to these particular disabilities."[8]

I would like to counter this mechanism of separation and exclusion that has been constructed in the name of the person with a thought, if not yet a practice, of the impersonal. Let me add at once that I don't intend it as a negation of what many see as noble, just, and worthy in the term *person*. On the contrary, I would like to assign the term *person* value and render it more effective. Yet such a project cannot avoid a radical critique of that process of depersonalization, or reification, that inheres in the very *dispositif* of the person, at least as it has functioned until now and continues to function. Moreover, such a thought of the impersonal doesn't emerge out of nowhere, though perhaps only today has it gained the urgency of a task that can't be put off any longer. The impersonal is already virtually, or implicitly, present in certain areas of philosophy, but also contemporary art, as well as certain practitioners of post-Freudian psychoanalysis, all of which have for some time been aiming to radically deconstruct personal identity.[9] Without attempting a full reconstruction of this entire hidden tradition (hidden insofar as it is covered over and drowned out by knowledges [*saperi*] and powers [*poteri*] associated with the person), in what follows, I'd like to sketch some features of the impersonal capable of giving us an outline for future work that can only be carried out by working together over a long period of time.

I'll begin by laying out three horizons of meaning or three semantic realms: justice, writing, and life. Each is linked to one of three names from twentieth-century philosophy. The first is Simone Weil. At the center of her work, there is an explicit critique of the hierarchical and exclusionary connection between rights and the person that I've been speaking about. "The notion of rights, by its very mediocrity, leads on naturally to that of the person, for rights are related to personal things. They are on that level. It is much worse still if the word 'personal' is added to the word 'rights,' thus implying the rights of the personality to what is called full expression."[10] What Weil grasps here is the limited and simultaneously private and privative character of rights, by connecting rights to the *dispositif* of the person. Once understood as the prerogative of certain subjects, rights exclude all those who do not belong to the same category. This explains why subjective rights, or personal rights, always have to do with, on the one hand, the economic exchange between measurable goods and, on the other, force. Only force is capable of imposing respect for a tendentious right upon those who don't agree with it.

Weil's conclusion is that if the person has always constituted the normative paradigm, the originary figure within which rights have expressed their own selective and exclusionary power [*potenza*], the only way to think universal justice, one that belongs to all and is for all, is from the perspective of the impersonal: "So far from its being his person, what is sacred in a human being is the impersonal in him. Everything which is impersonal in man is sacred, and nothing else."[11] If rights belong to the person, justice is situated in the realm of the impersonal. This is what turns the proper into the improper, the immune into the common. Only by dismantling the *dispositif* of the person will human beings be thought of as such, for what is at the same time absolutely singular and absolutely general about them: "Every man who has once touched the level of the impersonal is charged with a responsibility towards all human beings; to safeguard, not their persons, but whatever frail potentialities are hidden within them for passing over to the impersonal."[12] Weil is not asking us to repudiate the person; she does not make the impersonal the opposite of the personal, its simple negation. Instead, the impersonal is something within the person that inhibits the distinction and separation from all those who are not yet, no longer, or have never been, declared persons.

Where Simone Weil places the impersonal within the horizon of justice, Maurice Blanchot restores the impersonal to the regime of writing: Only writing, which shatters the interlocutory relation that within the dialogic word links the first person to the second, creates an opening into the impersonal. When he claims that "to write is to pass from 'I' to 'he,'" Blanchot is speaking not only of the writer's refusal of the possibility to speak in the first person in favor of the impersonality of a story told by the characters who themselves lack identities or qualities, as in Robert Musil's "man without qualities."[13] Blanchot also implies a de-centering of this narrative voice, employed first and foremost by Kafka, in which impersonality penetrates the very structure of the work, forcing the work to move continually outside itself. Two effects result that are bound together in the same movement: on the one hand, the lowering—that is, the true and proper aphonia—of the narrative voice, which is drowned out by the anonymous whir of events; on the other, the loss of identity by the subjects of the action with regard to themselves. Thus what is produced is a process of depersonalization that invests the entire surface of the text, lifting it out of its own margins and making the text spin on itself. This is what Blanchot defines elsewhere as the "relationship of the third kind," alluding to a dislocation of the entire perspectival field that we might compare to a true and proper leap in the epistemological paradigm.

Perhaps what matters most is that this movement toward depersonalization, one that Blanchot attempts in the field of writing, isn't just a mere theoretical position but is actually subjected to a sort of political experimentation. I have in mind a series of interventions, declarations, and stances—dating back primarily to the 1950s and 1960s, in which impersonality, or the exclusion of proper names, constitutes not only the form but the very content of the political act and its nonpersonal dimension (nonpersonal insofar as it is collective and common). As Blanchot writes to Sartre in December of 1960:

> Intellectuals . . . have also experienced—and this is not the least meaningful feature—a way of being together, and I am not thinking of the collective character of the Declaration, but of its impersonal force, the fact that all those who signed it certainly lent it their name, but without invoking their particular truth or their nominal fame. For them, the Declaration represented a certain anonymous community of names . . . [14]

The third horizon of meaning, the third semantic realm linked to impersonal paradigm, is that of life. In contemporary philosophy, this horizon can be found at the intersection of two names: Michel Foucault and Gilles Deleuze, each of whom, from the very beginning of their intellectual careers, and even at the level of biography, share a common deconstruction of the paradigm of the person. "Foucault himself," Deleuze writes:

> ... one did not grasp him exactly like a person. Even on insignificant occasions, when he entered a room, it was rather like a change of atmosphere, a kind of event, an electric or magnetic field, or what you will. This did not at all exclude gentleness or well-being, but it wasn't on the order of the person. It was an ensemble of intensities.[15]

What joins Deleuze and Foucault in a relationship that extends beyond simple friendship (because there is nothing personal about it) is their very reference to the third person—what Benveniste correctly defines as a non-person insofar as the power [*potenza*] of the impersonal crosses and limits the third person.[16] As Deleuze writes, "And then there's the emphasis on 'one,' in Foucault as in Blanchot: you have to begin by analyzing the third person. One speaks, one sees, one dies. There are still subjects, of course—but they're specks dancing in the dust of the visible and permutations in an anonymous babble."[17]

For Deleuze, this anonymous yet multiple, impersonal yet singular babble takes the form of life—or, better still, of *a* life (as one of his last texts is titled), because though life is common to all who live, it's never generic. Life is always someone's life; life never takes the exclusive (and excluding) form of the person because it works against such a divisive *dispositif*, and is one with itself. More than every other juridical subjectification, life constitutes the indivisible point at which man's being corresponds perfectly with the way in which the form (life) takes the shape of its own content. This is what Deleuze means when he connects life with what he calls a "plane of immanence." The phrase refers to the ever-shifting margin upon which immanence—life's being life—folds in on itself, eliding any figure of transcendence, any ulteriority to being such as it is of the living substance. In this sense, life, if taken on in all its impersonal power [*potenza*], is what contradicts the foundation of the hierarchical separation of humankind, and of man himself, into two superimposed, or subjugated, substances— the rational and the animal. It's no accident Deleuze places the enigmatic figure of "becoming animal" at the apex of the deconstruction of the idea of the person, in all of its philosophical, psychoanalytic, and political tonalities. Within a tradition that has always defined humankind according to its detachment and difference from the animal type (aside from the moments in which it animalizes a part of humanity because it's not human enough), claiming animality as our most essential nature, worth bringing back to light, breaks with the fundamental taboo that has always governed us. Against the doubling that the *dispositif* of the person presupposes, the animal in humankind, in every man and woman and all men and women, signifies multiplicity, plurality, and metamorphosis: "We do not become animal without a fascination for the pack, for the multiplicity. A fascination for the outside? Or is the multiplicity that fascinates us already related to a multiplicity dwelling within us?"[18] The "becoming animal" of humankind and within humankind means, and requires, a loosening of the metaphysical knot that is bound by the idea, and the practice, of the person in favor of a way of being human that no longer moves toward the thing but that finally coincides with only itself.

COMMUNITY AND VIOLENCE

Humankind has always seen community and violence as inherently related. Such a relation is, in fact, at the heart of the most important expressions of culture across history, be they of art, literature, or philosophy. The first graffiti etched in prehistoric grottoes depicted the human community through scenes of violence (hunting, sacrifice, battles). So too would war be the theme of the first great poem of Western civilization. Almost all world literatures, from the Hebrew to the Egyptian to the Indian, open with interhuman conflict and its images of violence and death to confirm for us a connection between community and violence that is seen as essential and originary. The same constitutive relation of community and violence is also evident when we speak of the origins of the human race. Not only is violence among humankind found at the beginning of history but community itself appears to have been founded by a homicidal violence. Cain's murder of Abel, which the Bible situates at the origin of human history, is echoed in classical mythology with Romulus's murder of Remus at Rome's founding. In each case the foundation of community seems to be tied to the blood of a cadaver that lies, abandoned, on the ground. The community itself lies under the open sky, atop a tomb that continually risks swallowing it whole. Nor should we forget that these originary homicides are represented not as simple murders but rather as fraternal ones involving brothers, as is the case in Greek tragedy, for instance, in the double murder of Eteocles and Polynices at the gates of Thebes. Herein will be found a detail that merits our attention: The blood that joins together a city is always the blood of a family—blood that, even before it is spilled, already links victim and executioner. It is undoubtedly this biological link of the communality of blood that seems to make the crime possible. Such a perspective strengthens the connection between community and violence. In the mythical representation of the origin, violence strikes the community not only from outside but also from within, from the center itself of what is "common." He who kills isn't a stranger but is rather a member of the community—indeed, the member who is closest both biologically and symbolically to the victim. Those that fight to the death do so not in spite of the fact but *because* they are brothers, because they are of the same blood and joined by the womb of the same mother.

René Girard is perhaps the contemporary author who has interpreted this founding myth most powerfully.[1] In his genealogical reconstruction, it is the brothers, indeed the twins, who are subjected to the most terrible sort of violence since violence, at its origin and along the course of its infinite history, is triggered by mimetic desire and by the fact that all human beings keep looking in the same direction, desiring the same thing. Furthermore, they don't desire the thing in itself but desire because everyone else desires it. Girard is saying that human beings fight to the death not because of the differences between them, as we still tend to believe ingenuously today, but because human beings are alike or even identical, like brothers, or even more so, twins. They kill each other not because they are too different but because they aren't different enough, which is to say they kill each other because of the excessive equality between them. When equality is too much, when it touches upon how desire is ordered, with everyone concentrating on the same object—then equality inescapably becomes reciprocal violence.

At the origin of modern political philosophy, Thomas Hobbes pushes this connection between reciprocal violence and equality to its tipping point, making it the base and the presupposition of his own system. It isn't some random external accident that produces an unbearable violence but community itself that does so. Moreover, violence is what human beings share most with each other, which is to say they share the possibility of killing and being killed. Our fundamental equality resides in this possibility of killing and being killed. Human beings are made equal, more than anything else, by the fact that all without distinction can be executioners as well as victims. They are, in the biological and technological resources that they have, so similar and so close to one another as to be always able to strike one another. Everyone has, at least potentially, the same capacity to kill and to be killed by anyone else. This is why what strikes fear into the heart of humankind in the scenario that Hobbes ushers in isn't the distance that divides men from each other but the equality that joins them together in the same shared condition. It isn't difference but indifference that brings human beings together, literally placing each in the hands of the other.

In all of the artistic, literary, philosophical, and theological reconstructions of the genesis of community, what sends the community spiraling into violence is surely indifference: the absence of the differential bar, which, making human beings distant from each other, keeps them from possibly being massacred.[2] The mass of people, which is to say the undifferentiated multitude, is doomed to destroy itself. This is the assumption of all the great myths of the foundation of community that modern political philosophy not only presupposes but sets down even more explicitly. Original man, who is dominated by the unlimited desire for everything and by the fear of being killed, can't help but destroy himself. What forces human beings to attack others is this fun house of mirrors in which everyone sees his or her own aggressiveness reflected in the other's glance. Sartre reduced it to the terrible expression that "Hell is other people," which is to say that others—namely, the community itself—are a hell for every "I."[3] What frightens human beings is a lack of boundaries, which places them in direct contact with others who are so similar to them that human beings cannot avoid letting loose sooner or later so as to assert themselves.

The heart of darkness, the obscure point of the originary community, is found in its unlimited nature, which makes it impossible to determine what community, in an absence of borders, actually means. Being everything that is and encompassing the entire space of life, community is not defined according to a principle of identity, be it toward what lies outside or what is contained within—this insofar as community, which is by its very nature limitless, doesn't have, so to speak, an outside. As a consequence, it doesn't have an inside either. Rather, what the originary community has is the lack of difference between inside and outside, and the violent reversal of one into the other.

If we return to two of the loftiest representations of the originary place whence we came, Dante's infernal woods and Vico's *ingens sylva*, we see that neither has limits: Nothing exists outside of either of them since the space of their "outside" is incorporated and dissolved in their "inside."[4] This explains why he who finds himself there cannot leave, why there is no outside in which one might find refuge, because the outside is nothing other than an imaginary projection of the inside. Here we find the pain and the unavoidable suffering that denotes the originary woods: not the impossibility of escape, but the absence of a place outside to escape to. Yet if the originary community has no external limits, as these writers who attempt to represent it understood it, then the community doesn't have any internal ones either. Those who inhabit it—that is, Dante's sinners, Vico's giants, or Hobbes's wolves—aren't separated by anything that can protect them from each other. They are literally exposed to what they have in common, to their being-nothing-other-than-community, a bare community stripped of every form. This is the reason why violence can be communicated freely until everything is made one through just such a communication of violence. What is communicated in the community is its violence, and its violence is the limitless possibility of such communication: "From the outset of this study," writes Girard, "I have regarded violence as something eminently communicable."[5] Contrary to the present-day rhetoric of limitless communication, modern and contemporary classics bring to light the risk of this excess of communication, of a communication that takes up within itself all of the space of the world, unifying it in a singular and sinister echo.

The essential relation of violence and communication means not only that violence is contagious but that violence resides in such a contagion. In a community without limits, in which no precise border exists between one and the other, violence takes on the fluid form of contamination. The material and symbolic channel for its flow is blood, because blood is the symbol itself of infection: "When violence is unloosed," Girard writes, "blood appears everywhere—on the ground, underfoot, forming great pools. Its very fluidity gives form to the contagious nature of violence."[6] The first blood, the blood of the first victim once spilled, infects the entire community, leading to reciprocal violence. It is the same connection between touch, contact, and contagion that Elias Canetti sees in the slight tremble that we feel, even today, when we sense that someone we do not know is touching us. What makes us pull back in this case is the threat raised against our individual identity, against the borders that circumscribe our body, which make our bodies different from others. It is this atavistic risk that hearkens back to a far-off origin that we cannot stand; one that makes us jump and shudder with irritation.[7] At issue here is the fear of falling back into the confusion and the promiscuity of the originary community, into that deadly communion of genus, blood, and sperm that Vico placed in the grand *selva*, which, caused by the universal flood, preceded human history. In this communion not only were human beings indistinguishable from others, massed together as they were without any differentiated form, but they were indistinguishable from animals, too, with whom they shared unlimited instincts and appetites. Vico called humans hulks, or "bestioni," to indicate their nearness to wild animals; similarly, Hobbes called them wolves. In the philosophical discourse of modernity, that originary community is literally unrepresentable because it lacks identity. Moreover, it seems doomed to break apart. For Hobbes, Locke, and Vico (as well as for Rousseau, despite his praise of the state of nature), life cannot be preserved in community. Life's communal dimension sweeps it away, which is to say by the lack of identity, individuality, and difference. The *munus* that circulates freely in community, more as a law of reciprocal gift giving, is seen as the poison that kills. Outside both the *logos* of discourse and the *nomos* of law, that antinomic community constitutes an intolerable threat for all its members.

Against this threat of undifferentiated community, modernity, in its dynamics and self-interpretation, erects an enormous apparatus of immunization. The concept of *immunitas* has to be contrasted directly with that of *communitas*. Both exist in relation to the term *munus*, from which they originate etymologically, though one has an affirmative meaning and the other negative. If the free circulation of the *munus* characterizes *communitas*, *immunitas* is what deactivates *communitas*.[8] *Immunitas* abolishes it, setting up new protective borders against what is outside the group as well as among its very own members. Ancient societies awarded the border a fundamental role of ordering when faced with a world given in common, which was doomed to chaos and reciprocal violence for exactly this reason. The only way to limit reciprocal violence seemed to be that of establishing solid borders, of marking insurmountable limits between one space and another. The linguist Émile Benveniste tells us of the symbolic importance of drawing borders between national and foreign territories, finding in this practice the most ancient role of *rex*, which is to say *regere fines*, or the sketching of impassable boundaries between one land and another. *Fines* and *limes* are words with which the ancient Romans indicated this urgent need to limit space to the point of making the "term" in fact a god, the god *Terminus*.[9]

From another part of the world, the Great Wall of China answers in kind to the same demand for protection. As Carl Schmitt pointed out so well, the *nomos* initially meant separation. The *nomos* is introduced by inscribing within land the distinction (as well as the opposition) between mine and yours, between ours and yours. From its origin onward, human civilization has practiced how to trace limits, terms, borders and raising walls between one territory and another.[10] What mattered for a politics often identified with the art of war was to impede trespassing by those who, breaking down protective terms, would have been able to "exterminate" the inhabitants of that territory. Yet if this activity of delimiting and confining characterizes human civilization from the very outset, the immunitary *dispositif* that modernity set in motion has quite another power as well. In a situation as chaotic and bloody as the one created at the end of the Middle Ages through the religious wars, the two *dispositifs* joined by state sovereignty and individual rights mark a clear passage from the regime of the "common" to that of the "proper" (or one's own). Hobbes and Locke are the first theoreticians of this general process of immunization that encompasses all modern political categories, from that of sovereignty to that of property as well as that of freedom. If for Hobbes the absolute state is born expressly out of the break with the originary community in favor of an order based on the vertical relation between every individual subject and the sovereign, for Locke it is instead the institution of property that separates the world into as many different parts as there are men to inhabit and work them. Against the boundlessness of the community, which is *absoluta* and *exlege,* the individual and the state are born under the sign of separation and autonomy with regard to what is internal to their own proper borders. By this time, we already see that impossible limits cover the entire world, dividing single states and the individuals that inhabit them. Only this division of what is common is able to give security to modern men and women.

Naturally, the price is high. In the case of Hobbes, the price consists of handing over all natural rights to the sovereign, thereby placing every political decision in his hands. For Locke, the price consists in moving away from the domination exercised by everyone over those things that are properly theirs to the increasing dependence on things when property becomes more important than the identity of the owner. This is what Marx will theorize in the concept of alienation and what Foucault takes up in the structural connection between the constitution of subjectivity and subjection: In the modern world, one becomes a subject only by subjecting oneself to something that at the same time makes us objects.[11] Moreover, this cost is implicit in a logic that, like that of immunization, functions only negatively by negating rather than affirming community. In medical terms we can say th immunity cures the disease thanks to poison, introjecting into the body the patient a fragment of the same disease from which it intends to protect itself. Here, the self-contradictory outcome of the entire immunitary paradigm that is activated in order to cope with the threat of the originary community is revealed. The violence of the *communitas* doesn't disappear at all but is incorporated into the same *dispositif* that ought to do away with it.

This is what Walter Benjamin singles out for example in the working of the law, understood not as the abolition but rather as the modern transposition of the ancient ritual of the sacrifice of a victim. Rather than being eliminated, violence is employed by power that should in fact be prohibiting violence. The immunitarian dialectic that is defined thusly can be summarized in three related passages. In the beginning there is always an act of violence, a war or a seizing of power that established the juridical order. Once founded, law then tends to exclude every other external violence from its workings. But law can do so only violently, by employing the same violence that it condemns. This explains Benjamin's conclusion that law is nothing other than violence against violence for the ultimate control of violence.[12] Violence is the hidden, repressed ground of every sovereign power, even when sovereign power appears to bear witness to its own right to life and death vis-à-vis subjects. Here, too, sovereign power, on the one hand, wields justice against those subjects who are unable to resist any of its decisions; on the other hand, sovereign power suspends justice when, in the case of exception, it oversteps the juridical order itself represented by sovereign power. Moreover, the sovereign is always free to declare war against other states, exporting violence from within its own borders outside. We should note as well that, from this point of view and at the exact moment of its constitution, sovereign power exercises its immunitarian role of preserving life, always keeping death in check with respect to life. Sovereign power makes death the horizon against which life can be identified, and then only negatively. In the case of the originary community without laws, modern society is certainly safeguarded from the immediate risk of extinction, but in a form that exposes the community to a potential violence even more intense because that violence is part of the same mechanism of protection.

Nevertheless, we are still only at the first stage of modern immunization. In its opening phase, the process of immunization is essentially meant to guarantee order against the conflict that risks reducing society to the chaos of the originary community. The function of immunization (as well as its intensity), however, changes noticeably in light of the biopolitical terms Foucault first employed to characterize modern processes of immunization.[13] When politics makes biological life the object of its own dynamics, the immunitary paradigm experiences a qualitative jump that turns it into the focal point of all the languages we use to describe individual and collective existence. Witness the increase in the importance that health, demographics, and urban planning undergo beginning at the end of the eighteenth century. This signals a substantial growth in immunization. At that moment human life, which is to say the body of individuals and populations, becomes what it is at stake in all political conflicts. What matters most is protecting human life from all contamination that puts at risk biological identity. Not only does medicine take on an increasingly political role but politics itself begins to speak in a medical voice, or better still, the voice of the surgeon. Every degeneration of the body is to be foreclosed anticipatorily by dispensing with the infected parts. Here more than anywhere else we can see the antinomic result when compared to the original intentions of immunization. Once the immunitary paradigm is combined with the *dispositifs* of nationalism and then racism, the paradigm becomes what determines and orders the destruction of life (let's recall again that immunization was born so as to protect life from its communitarian drift into chaos).[14] Nazism constituted the catastrophic apex of this reversal of biopolitics into its opposite, thanatopolitics. Once the life of a single population is presumed to be the ultimate and absolute value to defend and enhance, the clear result is that the lives of every other people or race can be sacrificed to the life of the single population. The immunitary paradigm now winds up producing a far greater violence through a series of discontinuous steps. Borders, we recall, were initially erected so as to limit the sovereign territory of single states as well as to protect the individual bodies of single citizens. At a certain point, however, they are understood to be thresholds within human life itself that allow the division of one part that is said to be superior from another that is considered inferior. This continues until a point is reached at which such a life is no longer worthy of being lived. The fifty million dead at the end of the Second World War represent the height of this apocalyptic process of immunization.

Contrary to the illusions of those who believed that with Nazism's defeat, as well as the defeat of communism forty years later, there would also come a weakening of the immunitary *dispositifs*, the last twenty years have seen them fortified anew. Similarly, the connection between politics and life today seems even firmer than in the past. Now more than ever, the demand for security has become truly obsessive. We aren't only dealing with an increase in the attention we pay to danger; rather, it is as if the usual relation between danger and protection has been reversed. No longer does the presence of risk demand protection but the demand for protection that artificially generates the sensation of risk. After all, hasn't the logic of insurance companies always been to produce an ever-greater fear of risk so as to increase the amount of protection? For the short circuit between protection and risk to encompass more of life, something else has to happen in how the world is shaped. Thus, recent decades have seen the introduction of that driving ensemble of events known as globalization. What globalization might actually refer to, what kinds of areas it covers, and what kinds of effects it has had are not the topics of this essay. What needs to be emphasized, rather, is the symbolic affinity of globalization with the features that the philosophic discourse of modernity has awarded the originary community, which is to say that chaotic and ungovernable world, an inferno, a state of nature, against which the modern political order is defined. In ways deeply similar to the originary community, globalization isn't so much a space as it is a nonspace in the sense that, overlapping with the entire globe, there is no outside and therefore no inside either. Just as is the case with the originary community, globalization knows no borders, no limits, and no terms. It is a totality that is fluid and spineless, so to speak, destined to push the world towards perennial mobilization. The global world is no longer to be differentiated between North and South, East and West, the Occident and the Orient. Instead, the global world sees these spaces as penetrating each other under the shock of continued migrations that break down every border. All of this happens while the flows of finance and information technologies move in real time across the entire globe. If the originary community appeared to Hobbes, Locke, and Vico as having no brakes at all, subjected as it was to overpowering impulses, nothing today seems able to put the brakes on globalization.

Of course, we shouldn't confuse reality with the image that theoreticians of globalization want to promote, even if such a distinction between reality and image is lessened in the universe of the virtual. What seems to be the unification of the world is rather a compulsory homologization that allows new and even more profound social, economic, and biological differences between continents, peoples, and ethnic groups to continue and indeed continually creates these differences. We might say that in the current model of globalization, the world is unified by its very separation. That is, the world is more united and more separated than ever before. Still, the dominant effect of globalization remains that of an infinite communication and also contamination between humankind, peoples, and languages that are already on top of one another, to the point that no longer any space exists whatsoever for any difference. It is the immunitary paradigm that fights against this uncontrollable contagion, a contagion that here too can be traced to the confusion of the originary community. The question concerns what in medical terms is called rejection of organs or transplants. The more ethnic, religious, and linguistic groups come into contact with each other, invading each other's respective spaces, the more do we find a movement toward a kind of exclusive attachment to one's own nation, party, or ethnic identity—in other words, toward a closing-off of identity. Never were so many walls erected than after the fall of the great symbolic wall of Berlin. Never more than today, when the world has been made one, does one feel the need to search out new lines of blockade and new networks of protection able to stop, or at least to delay, the invasion of others, the confusion between inside and outside, between internal and external, and between us and them.

The potentially catastrophic effect of such a state of affairs, which is to say the perverse interweaving between global and local, didn't wait around to show itself. September 11, 2001, and its ensuing events mark what can be defined as an immunitary crisis, by which I mean something not so distant from what Girard called a "sacrificial crisis": an explosion of the mechanism of victimary sacrifice that stretches like a spill across all of society, inundating it with blood. What has happened is a breakdown in the immunitary system, which until the 1980s had kept the world together through the apocalyptic threat of the atomic bomb. The end of that immunitary system, however, produced another that is even riskier because it is situated between an Islamic fundamentalism in search of revenge against the West and a Western fundamentalism that is just as fanatical, and which has shown itself of late to break apart in favor of a logic that is less suicidal. Once again, the excess of immunity seems to produce more violence than it is able to reduce. Now more than ever, universal rights seem to be a proclamation that lacks any real meaning. Now more than ever, at the culmination of the biopolitical epoch, does the first of these universal rights, that of life, appear to be betrayed by the millions who die because of hunger, disease, and war across a vast part of the world. The more globalization produces its poisoned fruit, the last of which is the dramatic economic crises of the present, the more frontiers seem to be blocked to those seeking shelter and sustenance outside of their own countries.

Yet attributing to globalization all the responsibility, or even considering stopping globalization somehow by restoring modernity's political borders, won't work. As was the case with the originary community when one tried to divide the space of the world into iron-clad frontiers, current immunitary attempts to neutralize global dynamics cannot but fail in the first instance because these attempts are impossible to mount and in the second because, even if they were possible, they are counterproductive. They would do nothing but disproportionately give new life to the conflict that they want to end. The real question is how to think biopolitics and globalization within the other. There is nothing more global than human life. The same world that is unified has taken on the form of a biological body that demands the maximum amount of care, one that doesn't tolerate wounds in any part of its body that are not reproduced immediately in every other part. This explains why the world's immunitary system isn't able to function by producing violence and death. Rather, the system must make itself the custodian and the producer of life. It must make itself not a barrier of separation but a filter of relations with what knocks plaintively from outside. The decisive point, and it is also the most difficult problem of them all, lies expressly in this 180-degree reversal of our perspective. The change in view has to first happen in our heads before it takes place in the real world.

Clearly, without any kind of immunitary system, the world, just as an individual human body, could not bear up. Yet as the immunitary system of our bodies also shows us, immunity is not to be understood only in contrast with community. We need to return to the element, the *munus*, understood as a donation, expropriation, and alteration, that holds together these two meanings. We need to be able to think together these principles of unity and difference, of community and immunity, which have battled each other across the centuries (and perhaps even millennia) in a struggle with no end or victory in sight for either side. It is of course true that community has always referred to identity and unity, just as immunity has referred to separation and difference. World history can be interpreted until today as the no-holds-barred struggle between these juxtaposed principles. Now is the time, however, to put community and immunity in a reciprocal relation, to have community refer to difference and immunity to contamination, which is what happens in our bodies and in all organ transplants. It is what so-called immunitary tolerance allows for. Of course, translating what might appear to be, and in fact are, philosophical formulas into reality is anything but easy. Yet as the history of thought as well the history of humankind demonstrates, for something to be made to happen, one needs to have it gestate over a long period. This is the direction that my work, woven together with the work of many others, has followed of late.

NOTES

THE LAW OF COMMUNITY

1. [Throughout the essay, as elsewhere, Esposito plays on the varied meanings of the Italian *colpa* as "misdeed" or "offense," and "guilt." See his chapter "Guilt" in Roberto Esposito, *Communitas: The Origin and Destiny of Community*, trans. Timothy Campbell (Stanford, Calif.: Stanford University Press, 2010), 41–61, 159n6.—*Trans.*]

2. See Bernard Baas, "Le corps du délit," in *Politique et modernité*, ed. Georges Leyenberger (Paris: Editions Osiris, 1992). [Elsewhere, Esposito refers to the double meaning of *delinquere* as both "to be lacking" and "to be at fault." See Esposito, *Communitas*, 50n25, 50n160.—*Trans.*]

3. Roberto Esposito, *Categorie dell'impolitico* (Bologna: Il Mulino, 1988), 245–312. [Translation by Fordham University Press forthcoming.—*Trans.*]

4. Jean-Jacques Rousseau, *The Social Contract and the First and Second Discourses*, ed. Susan Dunn (New Haven, Conn.: Yale University Press, 2002), 162.

5. Jean-Jacques Rousseau, *Rousseau, Judge of Jean-Jacques: Dialogues*, trans. Judith Bush, Christopher Kelly, and Roger Masters (Hanover, N.H.: University Press of New England, 1990), 118.

6. Bronislaw Baczko, *Rousseau: Solitude et communauté* (Paris: Mouton, 1974), 263.

7. Émile Durkheim, "Le 'Contrat social' de Rousseau," *Revue de métaphysique et de morale* 25 (1918), 13–139.

8. [The "impolitical," sometimes translated into English as the "unpolitical," is one of Esposito's most operative and discussed terms. The "impolitical" refers to the unrepresentable origin of politics. See Esposito, *Categorie dell'impolitico*—*Trans.*]

9. Robert Derathé, *Rousseau e la scienza politica del suo tempo* (Bologna: Il Mulino, 1993), 305.

10. Rousseau, *The Social Contract*, 181.

11. Paul Monique Vernes, *La ville, la fête, la démocratie: Rousseau et les illusions de la communauté* (Paris: Payot, 1978).

12. See, for example, in a different context: Jean Starobinski, *Jean-Jacques Rousseau, Transparency and Obstruction* (Chicago: University of Chicago Press 1988).

13. Rousseau, *The Social Contract*, 201.

14. Jean-Jacques Rousseau, *Émile; or, On Education*, trans. Allan Bloom (New York: Basic Books, 1979) 221–22.

15. Immanuel Kant, "Bemerkungen zu den Beobachtungen über das Gefühl des Schönen und Erhabenen," in *Kant Gesammelte Schriften* (Berlin: Akademie-Ausgabe, 1902), 44.

16. Immanuel Kant, "What Does It Mean to Orient Oneself in Thinking?," in *Religion within the Boundaries of Mere Reason and Other Writings*, ed. Allen Wood and George Di Giovanni (Cambridge, UK: Cambridge University Press, 1998), 12.

17. Lucien Goldmann, *Introduction à la philosophie de Kant* (Paris: Gallimard, 1967).

18. Hannah Arendt, *Lectures on Kant's Political Philosophy*, ed. Ronald Beiner (Chicago: University of Chicago Press, 1992), 75.

19. See for example, Aldo Masullo, *La comunità come fondamento* (Naples Libreria Scientifica Editrice, 1965).

20. Immanuel Kant, "Religion within the Boundaries of Mere Reason," in *Religion and Rational Theology*, ed. Allen Wood (Cambridge, UK: Cambridge University Press, 1996), 111. [The Italian translation that Esposito cites refers to "an ethical community." See Immanuel Kant, "La religione nei limiti della semplice ragione," in *Scritti morali*, ed. P. Chiodi (Turin: UTET, 1970).—*Trans.*]

21. Alexis Philonekno, *Théorie et praxis dans la pensée morale et politique de Kant et de Fichte en 1973* (Paris: Vrin, 1988), 28–29.

22. Kant, "What Does It Mean to Orient Oneself in Thinking?," 106.

23. Jean-François Lyotard, *The Differend: Phrases in Dispute*, trans. Georges Van Den Abeelle (Minneapolis: University of Minnesota Press, 1988).

24. Immanuel Kant, "A Renewed Attempt to Answer the Question: 'Is the Human Race Continually Improving?,'" in *Political Writings*, ed. H. S. Reiss (Cambridge, UK: Cambridge University Press, 1991), 177–90.

25. Immanuel Kant, "Perpetual Peace: A Philosophical Sketch," in *Political Writings*, ed. H. S. Reiss (Cambridge, UK: Cambridge University Press, 1991), 112.

26. Immanuel Kant, "Idea for a Universal History with a Cosmopolitan Purpose," in *Political Writings*, ed. H. S. Reiss (Cambridge, UK: Cambridge University Press, 1991), 41–53.

27. Immanuel Kant, "Conjectural Beginning of Human History," in *The Cambridge Edition of the Works of Immanuel Kant: Anthropology, History, and Education* (Cambridge, UK: Cambridge University Press, 2009), 169.

28. Again, see Baas, "Le corps du délit."

29. Kant, "Conjectural Beginning of Human History," 175.

30. Ernst Cassirer, *The Question of Jean-Jacques Rousseau*, trans. Peter Gay (Bloomington: Indiana University Press, 1975).

31. Jean Luc Nancy, *L'impératif catégorique* (Paris: Flammarion, 1983).

32. Kant, "Religion within the Boundaries of Mere Reason," 112.

33. Immanuel Kant, "Critique of Practical Reason," in *Practical Philosophy*, ed. Mary J. Gregor (Cambridge, UK: Cambridge University Press, 1996), 199–200. [For alternative translations of *Selbstliebe* ("self-love") and *Eigenliebe* (as "love for oneself"), see Immanuel Kant, *Critique of Practical Reason*, trans. Werner S. Pluhar (Indianapolis, Ind.: Hackett, 2002), 96.—*Trans.*]

34. [Here, Esposito plays on the verbal adjective *finito*, which means at once "complete," "finished," "exhausted," and "finite."—*Trans.*]

35. Martin Heidegger, "The Question concerning the Human Essence and the Authentic Result of the Kantian Ground-Laying," in *Kant and the Problem of Metaphysics*, trans. Richard Taft (Bloomington: Indiana University Press: 1997), 151.

36. Martin Heidegger, *Being and Time*, trans. Joan Stambaugh (Albany: SUNY Press, 1996), 254.

37. ["Being guilty constitutes the being that we call care." Heidegger, *Being and Time*, 264.—*Trans.*]

38. Heidegger, *Being and Time*, 167.

39. Ibid., 111–12.

40. ["But if fateful Da-sein essentially exists as being-in-the-world in being-with others, its occurrence is an occurrence-with and is determined as *destiny*. With this term, we designate the occurrence of the community, of a people. Destiny is not composed of individual fates, nor can being-with-one-another be conceived of as the mutual occurrence of several subjects. These fates are already guided beforehand in being-with-one-another in the same world and in the resoluteness for definite possibilities." Heidegger, *Being and Time*, 352.—*Trans.*]

41. Heidegger, *Being and Time*, 115.

42. [Here Esposito refers to Arthur Rimbaud's famous proclamation "je est un autre" ("I is another").—*Trans.*]

MELANCHOLY AND COMMUNITY

1. Jean-Jacques Rousseau, *Émile; or, On Education*, trans. Allan Bloom (New York: Basic Books, 1979), 222.

2. Martin Heidegger, *The Fundamental Concepts of Metaphysics: World, Finitude, Solitude*, trans. William McNeill and Nicholas Walker (Bloomington: Indiana University Press, 1995), 183.

3. Martin Heidegger, *Being and Time*, trans. Joan Stambaugh (Albany: SUNY Press, 1996), 113.

IMMUNITARY DEMOCRACY

1. [The Italian *comprendere* means both "to understand" and "to include," as does its English equivalent.—*Trans.*]

2. Esposito, *Communitas*.

3. Ferdinand Tönnies, *Community and Civil Society*, trans. José Harris (Cambridge, UK: Cambridge University Press, 2001).

4. Roberto Esposito, *Immunitas: Protezione e negazione della vita* (Turin: Einaudi, 2002).

5. For one of the few positive exceptions to this, see Massimo Cacciari, *L'arcipelago* (Milan: Adelphi, 1997).

6. Georges Bataille, *The College of Sociology (1937–1939)*, ed. Denis Hollier (Minneapolis: University of Minnesota Press, 1988).

7. Helmuth Plessner, *The Limits of Community: A Critique of Social Radicalism*, trans. Andrew Wallace (New York: Humanity Books, 1999).

8. Elias Canetti, *Crowds and Power*, trans. Carol Stewart (New York: Farrar, Straus, and Giroux, 1960), 15–16.

9. Arnold Gehlen, *Man, His Nature and Place in the World*, trans. Clare McMillan and Karl Pillemer (New York: Columbia University Press, 1988).

10. Ubaldo Fadini, ed., *Desiderio di vita: Conversazione sulle metamorfosi dell'uomo* (Milan: Mimesis, 1995).

11. Niklas Luhmann, *Social Systems*, trans. John Bednarz (Stanford, Calif.: Stanford University Press, 1995), 382.

12. Ibid., 403.

13. Alfred I. Tauber, *The Immune Self: Theory or Metaphor?* (Cambridge: Cambridge University Press, 1994).

14. Georges Bataille, *La congiura sacra*, ed. Roberto Esposito and Marina Galletti (Turin: Bollati Boringhieri, 1997).

15. [The Latin *ontologia*, which is the same as the Italian, appears in the original text in italics.—*Trans.*]

16. Jean Luc Nancy, *The Sense of the World*, trans. Jeffrey Librett (Minneapolis: University of Minnesota Press, 1997).

FREEDOM AND IMMUNITY

1. [The Italian title of this essay is "Libertà e immunità." The Italian *libertà* means both "liberty" and "freedom." I have translated it throughout the essay as *freedom*, following the English translations of the term among Esposito's interlocutors in this

essay, Hannah Arendt, René Char, Osip Mandelstam, Jean-Luc Nancy, and Arthur Rimbaud.—*Trans.*]

2. Simone Weil, "The Power of Words," in *Selected Essays 1934–1943* (London Oxford University Press, 1962), 163.

3. Esposito, *Communitas*.

4. Nancy, *The Experience of Freedom*.

5. Theodore Adorno, *Negative Dialectics* (London: Routledge, 1973), 265.

6. Henri Broch, "L'assoluto terrestre," in *Oltre la politica: Antologia del pensiero dell' 'impolitico,'* ed. Roberto Esposito. (Milan: Mondadori, 1996).

7. We ought not lose sight of the transitive modality of the verb *to participate*—to make someone a participant in something; to communicate; to share.

8. Hannah Arendt, "What Is Freedom?," *Between Past and Future* (New York: Penguin, 1961).

9. Osip Mandelstam, "The Twilight of Freedom," in *The Selected Poems of Osip Mandelstam*, trans. Clarence Brown and William Stanley (New York: New York Review of Books, 2004), 22.

10. Nancy, *Experience of Freedom*.

11. Luigi Pareyson, *Ontologia della libertà* (Turin: Einaudi, 1995).

12. Arendt, "What Is Freedom?," 167.

13. Arthur Rimbaud, "Letter to Georges Izambard: Charleville, November 2, 1870," in *I Promise to Be Good: The Letters of Arthur Rimbaud*, trans. Wyatt Mason (New York: Random House, 2004), 24.

14. René Char, *Oeuvres Complètes* (Paris: Gallimard, 1983), 733.

15. René Char, *Leaves of Hypnos* (New York: Grossman, 1973), 131.

IMMUNIZATION AND VIOLENCE

1. [Here Esposito refers to the George W. Bush administration's "War on Terror" and the United States–led military campaigns in Iraq and Afghanistan that began in response to the attacks of September 11, 2001.—*Trans.*]

BIOPOLITICS AND PHILOSOPHY

1. Roberto Esposito, *Bios: Biopolitics and Philosophy*, trans. Timothy Campbell (Minneapolis: University of Minnesota Press, 2008); Laura Bazzicalupo and Roberto Esposito, eds., *Politica della vita* (Rome; Bari: Laterza, 2003); Antonella Cutro, *Biopolitica* (Verona: Ombre Corte, 2005); "Biopolitica," *Filosofia Politica* 1 (2006); Adriano Vinale, ed., *Biopolitica e democrazia* (Milan: Mimesis, 2007); Ottavio Marzocca, *Perché il governo* (Rome: Manifestolibri, 2007).

2. Peter Sloterdijk, *Die letzte Jugel: Zu einer philosophischen Geschichte der terrestrischen Globalisierung* (Frankfurt: Suhrkamp, 2002).

3. Michel Foucault, *The Birth of Biopolitics: Lectures at the Collège de France, 1978–1979*, trans. Graham Burchell (New York: Palgrave Macmillan, 2008); Michel Foucault, *Security, Territory, Population: Lectures at the Collège de France, 1977–78* (New York: Palgrave Macmillan, 2007).

4. Michel Foucault, *Society Must Be Defended: Lectures at the Collège de France, 1975–76*, trans. David Macey (New York: Picador, 2003).

5. Esposito, *Immunitas*.

6. Friedrich Nietzsche, *Sämtliche Briefe*, vol. 5.2 (Munich and Berlin: de Gruyter, 1986), 445. [Cited in Robert Holub, "Dialectic of the Biological Enlightenment: Nietzsche, Degeneration, and Eugenics," in *Practicing Progress: The Promise and Limitations of Enlightenment* (Amsterdam: Rodopi, 2007), 182.—*Trans.*]

7. Emmanuel Lévinas, "Some Thoughts on the Philosophy of Hitlerism," in *Unforeseen History*, trans. Nidra Poller (Bloomington: University of Indiana Press, 2004).

8. Hans Friedrich Karl Gunther, *Humanitas* (Munich: Lehmanns, 1937).

9. Karl Binding and Alfred Hoche, *Permitting the Destruction of Unworthy Life* (Terre Haute, Ind.: National Legal Center for the Medically Dependent and Disabled, 1992); Karl Binding and Alfred Hoche, *Die Freigabe der Vernichtung lebensunwerten Lebens: Ihr Mass und ihre Form* (Leipzig: Meiner, 1920).

10. Adriana Cavarero, *Horrorism: Naming Contemporary Violence* (New York: Columbia University Press, 2009).

11. Gilles Deleuze and Félix Guattari, *What Is Philosophy?*, trans. Hugh Tomlinson and Graham Burchell (New York: Columbia University Press, 1994).

NAZISM AND US

1. Simona Forti, *Il totalitarismo* (Rome; Bari: Laterza, 2001).

2. Cited in Robert Jay Lifton, *The Nazi Doctors: Medical Killing and the Psychology of Genocide* (New York: Basic Books, 1986), 31.

3. Erwin Baur, Eugen Fischer, and Fritz Lenz, *Grundriss der menschlichen Erblichkeitslehre und Rassenhygiene* (Munich: Lehmann, 1931), 417–18.

4. Adolf Hitler, *Mein Kampf*, trans. Ralph Manheim (1943; Boston: Houghton Mifflin, 1971), 257.

5. Rudolf Ramm, *Ärztliche Rechts- und Standeskunde: Der Arzt als Gesundheitserzieher* (Berlin: De Gruyter, 1943), 178. Also cited in Lifton, *The Nazi Doctors*, 30.

6. Ramm, *Ärztliche Rechts- und Standeskunde*, 156.

7. Paul Weindling, *Health, Race, and German Politics between National Unification and Nazism, 1870–1945* (Cambridge, UK: Cambridge University Press, 1989), 220.

8. Giorgio Agamben, *Homo Sacer: Sovereign Power and Bare Life* (Stanford, Calif.: Stanford University Press, 1998), 143.

9. Hans Reiter, "'La biologie dans la gestion de l'État,'" in *État et santé: L'image héréditaire de l'homme*, ed. Otmar von Verscheur, Leonardo Conti, and Hans Reiter (Paris: Sorlot, 1942), 51.

10. Raffaella De Franco, *In nome di Ippocrate: Dall'Olocausto medico nazista all'etica della sperimentazione contemporanea* (Milan: Angeli, 2001).

11. Cited in Benno Muller-Hill, *Murderous Science: Elimination by Scientific Selection of Jews, Gypsies, and Others; Germany 1933–1945* (Oxford, UK: Oxford University Press, 1988), 102.

12. Ernst Klee, *Auschwitz, die NS-Medizin und ihre Opfer* (Frankfurt am Main: S. Fischer, 1997).

13. Robert Proctor, *The Nazi War on Cancer* (Princeton, N.J.: Princeton University Press, 1999).

14. Lifton, *The Nazi Doctors*, 139.

15. [Much of this discussion is found in Robert Esposito, "Thanatopolitics (The Cycle of *Genos*)," chap. 4 in *Bios: Biopolitics and Philosophy*, trans. Timothy Campbell (Minneapolis: University of Minnesota Press, 2008), 111–17.—*Trans.*]

16. Foucault, *Society Must Be Defended*, 239–63.

17. Esposito, *Immunitas*.

18. Andrzej Kaminski, *I campi di concentramento dal 1896 a oggi* (Turin: Bollati Boringhieri, 1997), 84–85.

19. Ibid., 94.

20. Adolf Hitler, *Libres propos sur la guerre et la paix recueillis sur l'ordre de Martin Bormann* (Paris: Flammarion, 1952), 1:321.

21. Christopher Browning, *The Path to Genocide: Essays on Launching the Final Solution* (Cambridge, UK: Cambridge University Press, 1992), 145–58.

POLITICS AND HUMAN NATURE

1. Sartre's essay "Existentialism is a Humanism" was written in the same year as "Letter on Humanism."

2. Martin Heidegger, "Letter on Humanism," in *Basic Writings*, ed. David Farrell Krell (New York: Harper Collins, 1977), 233–34.

3. Ibid., 227.

4. Ibid.

5. Ibid., 230.

6. Ibid., 247.

7. Giovanni Pico della Mirandola, *On the Dignity of Man*, trans. Charles Glenn Wallis, Paul J. W. Miller, and Douglas Carmichael (Indianapolis, Ind.: Hackett, 1998), 6.

8. Jean-Paul Sartre, *Existentialism Is a Humanism*, trans. Carol Macomber (New Haven, Conn.: Yale University Press, 2007), 36.

9. Ibid., 22.

10. Nietzsche, *Sämtliche Briefe*, 445. [Cited in Holub, "Dialectic of the Biological Enlightenment, 182.—*Trans.*]

11. Peter Sloterdijk, *Reglen für den Menschenpark* (Frankfurt am Main: Suhrkamp, 1999).

12. George Canguilhem, *The Normal and the Pathological*, trans. Carolyn R. Fawcett (New York: Zone Books, 1998).

13. Giorgio Agamben, et al., eds., *La natura umana* (Rome: DeriveApprodi, 2004).

14. Dominique Lecourt, *Humain, posthumain: La tecnique et la vie* (Paris: Presses Universitaires de France, 2003).

15. Esposito, *Immunitas*.

16. Roberto Marchesini, *Post-human: Verso nuovi modelli di esistenza* (Turin: Bollati Boringhieri, 2002).

TOTALITARIANISM OR BIOPOLITICS: TOWARD A PHILOSOPHICAL INTERPRETATION OF THE TWENTIETH CENTURY

1. Augusto Del Noce, *L'interpretazione transpolitica della storia contemporanea* (Naples: Guida, 1982).

2. Hannah Arendt, *The Origins of Totalitarianism* (1968; Orlando: Harcourt, 1994); Jacob Laib Talmon, *The Origins of Totalitarian Democracy* (Secker and Warburg: London, 1952).

3. Arendt, *The Origins of Totalitarianism*, 157.

4. Francois Furet, *The Passing of an Illusion: The Idea of Communism in the Twentieth Century*, trans. Deborah Furet (Chicago: University of Chicago Press, 1999).

5. Raymond Aron, *Democracy and Totalitarianism (A Theory of Political Regimes)*, trans. Valence Ionescu (New York: Praeger, 1968).

6. Marcel Gauchet, "L'expérience totalitaire et la pensée de la politique," in *Retour du politique* (Paris: Esprit, 1976); Claude Lefort, *L'invention démocratique: Les limites de la domination totalitaire* (Paris: Fayard, 1981).

7. Foucault, *Security, Territory, Population*.

8. Michel Foucault, "Nietzsche, Genealogy, History," *The Essential Foucault*, ed. Paul Rabinow and Nikolas Rose (1971; New York: The New Press, 2003), 357–69.

9. Ernst Nolte, *Der europäische Bürgerkrieg 1917–1945: Nationalsozialismus und Bolschewismus* (Berlin: Propyläen, 1987).

10. Lévinas, "Some Thoughts on the Philosophy of Hitlerism," 18.

11. Carl Schmitt, *The Crisis of Parliamentary Democracy*, trans. Ellen Kennedy (Cambridge, Mass.: MIT Press, 1988).

12. Foucault, *The Birth of Biopolitics*.

13. Giuseppe Duso, *Oltre la democrazia: Un itinerario attraverso i classici* (Rome: Carocci, 2004); Fabrizio Elefante, *La fiducia nella democrazia* (Milan: IPOC, 2006).

14. Roberto Esposito, *Terza persona: Politica della vita e filosofia dell'impersonale* (Turin: Einaudi, 2007).

TOWARD A PHILOSOPHY OF THE IMPERSONAL

1. Luigi Ferrajoli, *Diritti fondamentali* (Rome-Bari: Laterza, 2001); Stefano Rodotà, *La vita e le regole: Tra diritto e non diritto* (Milan: Feltrinelli, 2006).

2. Martha Nussbaum, *Sex and Social Justice* (Oxford, UK: Oxford University Press, 1999).

3. Roberta de Monticelli, ed., *La persona: Apparenza e realtà; Testi fenomenologici 1911–1933* (Milan: Cortina, 2000).

4. On this, see Remo Bodei, *Destini personali: L'età della coloniazzazione delle coscienze* (Milan: Feltrinelli, 2002).

5. Yan Thomas, "Le sujet du droit, la personne et la nature," *Le débat* 100 (1998), 85–107.

6. Thomas Hobbes, *Leviathan*, trans. Edwin Curley (Indianapolis, Ind.: Hackett, 1994), 101.

7. Jacques Maritain, *The Rights of Man and Natural Law* (New York: Charles Scribner's Sons, 1943), 55.

8. Peter Singer, *Writings on an Ethical Life* (New York: HarperCollins, 2000), 193.

9. See Enrica Petrini, "Fuori della persona," *Filosofia Politica* 3 (2007); Pietro Montani, *Bioestetica* (Rome: Carocci, 2007).

10. Simone Weil, "Human Personality," in *Simone Weil: An Anthology*, trans. Sian Miles (New York: Grove Press, 1986), 64.

11. Ibid., 55.

12. Ibid., 58.

13. Maurice Blanchot, *The Infinite Conversation* (Minneapolis: University of Minnesota Press, 1993), 380.

14. Maurice Blanchot, *Political Writings, 1953–1993*, trans. Kevin Hart (New York: Fordham University Press, 2010), 36.

15. Gilles Deleuze, *Negotiations*, trans. Martin Joughin (New York: Columbia University Press, 1995), 99.

16. Émile Benveniste, *Problèmes de linguistique générale* (Paris: Gallimard, 1976), 230–32.

17. Deleuze, *Negotiations*, 108.

18. Deleuze and Guattari, *A Thousand Plateaus: Capitalism and Schizophrenia*, trans. Brian Massumi (Minneapolis: University of Minnesota Press, 1978), 239–40.

COMMUNITY AND VIOLENCE

1. Rene Girard, *Violence and the Sacred*, trans. Patrick Gregory (Baltimore, Md.: Johns Hopkins University Press, 1984).

2. Consider, for instance, the myth of the Tower of Babel and the confusion of tongues that renders individual voices indistinct.

3. Jean-Paul Sartre, *No Exit, and Three Other Plays* (New York: Vintage, 1989).

4. Roberto Esposito, *Pensiero vivente: Origine e attualità della filosofia italiana* (Turin: Einaudi, 2010).

5. Girard, *Violence and the Sacred*, 31.

6. Ibid., 35.

7. Canetti, *Crowds and Power*, 15–16.

8. Esposito, *Immunitas*; Esposito, *Communitas*.

9. Émile Benveniste, *Indo-European Language and Society* (Coral Gables, Fl.: University of Miami Press, 1973).

10. Carl Schmitt, *The Nomos of the Earth in the International Law of the Jus Publicum Europaeum*, trans. G. L. Ulmen (New York: Telos, 2003).

11. Michel Foucault, *The Hermeneutics of the Subject*, trans. Graham Burchel (New York: Picador, 2005).

12. Walter Benjamin, "Critique of Violence," in *Selected Writings*, vol. 1, *1913–1926*, trans. Marcus Bullock and Michael Jennings (1996).

13. Michel Foucault, *Society Must Be Defended*.

14. Esposito, *Bios*.

BIBLIOGRAPHY

Accarino, Bruno, ed. *Ratio imaginis: Uomo e mondo nell'antropologia filosofica.* Florence: Ponte alle Grazie, 1991.

Adorno, Theodore. *Negative Dialectics.* London: Routledge, 1973.

Agamben, Giorgio. *Homo Sacer: Sovereign Power and Bare Life.* Stanford, Calif.: Stanford University Press, 1998.

Agamben, Giorgio, et al., eds. *La natura umana.* Rome: DeriveApprodi, 2004.

Arendt, Hannah. *Lectures on Kant's Political Philosophy.* Ed. Ronald Beiner. Chicago: University of Chicago Press, 1992.

———. *The Origins of Totalitarianism.* 1968. Orlando: Harcourt, 1994.

———. "What Is Freedom?" In *Between Past and Future,* 143-72. New York: Penguin, 1961.

Aron, Raymond. *Democracy and Totalitarianism (A Theory of Political Regimes).* Translated by Valence Ionescu. New York: Praeger, 1968.

Baas, Bernard. "Le corps du délit." In *Politique et modernité,* edited by Georges Leyenberger. Paris: Editions Osiris, 1992.

Baczko, Bronislaw. *Rousseau: Solitude et communauté.* Paris: Mouton, 1974.

Bataille, Georges. *The College of Sociology (1937-1939).* Edited by Denis Hollier. Minneapolis: University of Minnesota Press, 1988.

———. *La congiura sacra.* Edited by Roberto Esposito and Marina Galletti. Turin: Bollati Boringhieri, 1997.

Baur, Erwin, Eugen Fischer, and Fritz Lenz. *Grundriss der menschlichen Erblichkeitslehre und Rassenhygiene.* Munich: Lehmann, 1931.

Bazzicalupo, Laura, and Roberto Esposito, eds. *Politica della vita.* Rome: Laterza, 2003.

Benjamin, Walter. "Critique of Violence." In *Selected Writings.* Vol. 1, *1913-1926,* translated by Marcus Bullock and Michael Jennings, 236-52. Cambridge, Mass: Belknap Press of Harvard University, 1996.

Benveniste, Émile. *Indo-European Language and Society*. Coral Gables, Fl.: University of Miami Press, 1973.

———. *Problèmes de linguistique générale*. Paris: Gallimard, 1976.

Binding, Karl, and Alfred Hoche. *Die Freigabe der Vernichtung lebensunwerten Lebens: Ihr Mass und ihre Form*. Leipzig: Meiner, 1920.

Binswanger, Ludwig. *Melancholie und Manie: Phanomenologische Studien*. Pfullingen: Neske, 1960.

Blanchot, Maurice. *The Infinite Conversation*. Minneapolis: University of Minnesota Press, 1993.

———. *Political Writings, 1953–1993*. Translated by Kevin Hart. Bronx, New York: Fordham University Press, 2010.

Blome, Kurt. *Arzt im Kampf: Erlebnisse und Gedanken*. Leipzig: Barth, 1941.

Bodei, Remo. *Destini personali: L'età della coloniazzazione delle coscienze*. Milan: Feltrinelli, 2002.

Bonnefoy, Yves. *Rimbaud*. New York: Harper and Row, 1973.

Bortolini, Matteo. *L'immunità necessaria: Talcott Parsons e la sociologia della modernità*. Rome: Meltemi, 2005.

Broch, Henri. "L'assoluto terrestre." In *Oltre la politica: Antologia del pensiero dell' 'impolitico.'* Edited by Roberto Esposito, 129–46. Milan: Mondadori, 1996.

Browning, Christopher. *The Path to Genocide: Essays on Launching the Final Solution*. Cambridge, UK: Cambridge University Press, 1992.

Burton, Robert. *The Anatomy of Melancholy*. London: E. P. Dutton, 1932.

Cacciari, Massimo. *L'arcipelago*. Milan: Adelphi, 1997.

———. *Geo-filosofia dell'Europa*. Milan: Adelphi, 1997.

Canetti, Elias. *Crowds and Power*. Translated by Carol Stewart. New York: Farrar, Straus, and Giroux, 1960.

Canguilhem, George. *The Normal and the Pathological*. Translated by Carolyn R. Fawcett. New York: Zone Books, 1998.

Cassirer, Ernst. *The Question of Jean-Jacques Rousseau*. Translated by Peter Gay. Bloomington: Indiana University Press, 1975.

Cavarero, Adriana. *Horrorism: Naming Contemporary Violence*. New York: Columbia University Press, 2009.

Char, René. *Leaves of Hypnos*. New York: Grossman, 1973.

———. *Oeuvres Complètes*. Paris: Gallimard, 1983.

Colangelo, Carmelo. *Limite e melanconia: Kant, Heidggger, Blanchot*. Naples: Loffredo, 1998.

Cutro, Antonella. *Biopolitica*. Verona: Ombre Corte, 2005.

De Franco, Raffaella. *In nome di Ippocrate: Dall'Olocausto medico nazista all'etica della sperimentazione contemporanea*. Milan: Angeli, 2001.

De Monticelli, Roberta, ed. *La persona: Apparenza e realtà; Testi fenomenologici 1911–1933*. Milan: Cortina, 2000.

Del Noce, Augusto. *L'interpretazione transpolitica della storia contemporanea.* Naples: Guida, 1982.

Deleuze, Gilles. *Negotiations.* New York: Columbia University Press, 1995.

Deleuze, Gilles, and Félix Guattari. *A Thousand Plateaus: Capitalism and Schizophrenia.* Translated by Brian Massumi. Minneapolis: University of Minnesota Press, 1978.

———. *What Is Philosophy?* Translated by Hugh Tomlinson and Graham Burchell. New York: Columbia University Press, 1994.

Derathé, Robert. *Rousseau e la scienza politica del suo tempo.* Bologna: Il Mulino, 1993.

Derrida, Jacques. "Autoimmunity: Real and Symbolic Suicides; A Dialogue with Jacques Derrida." In *Philosophy in a Time of Terror: Dialogues with Jurgen Habermas and Jacques Derrida,* edited by Giovanna Borradori, 85–136. Chicago: University of Chicago Press, 2003.

D'Ippolito, Bianca Maria. *Geometria e malinconia: Mathesis e meditatio nel pensiero moderno.* Genova: Marietti, 1992.

Durkheim, Émile. "Le 'Contrat social' de Rousseau." *Revue de métaphysique et de morale* 25 (1918): 13–139.

Duso, Giuseppe. *Oltre la democrazia: Un itinerario attraverso i classici.* Rome: Carocci, 2004.

Elefante, Fabrizio. *La fiducia nella democrazia.* Milan: IPOC, 2006.

Esposito, Roberto. *Bios: Biopolitics and Philosophy.* Translated by Timothy Campbell. Minneapolis: University of Minnesota Press, 2008.

———. *Categorie dell'impolitico.* Bologna: Il Mulino, 1988.

———. *Communitas: The Origin and Destiny of Community.* Translated by Timothy Campbell. Stanford, Calif.: Stanford University Press, 2010.

———. *Immunitas: Protezione e negazione della vita.* Turin: Einaudi, 2002.

———. *Pensiero vivente: Origine e attualità della filosofia italiana.* Turin: Einaudi, 2010.

———. "Presentazione." *Filosofia politica* 1 (2006): 3–9.

———. *Terza persona: Politica della vita e filosofia dell'impersonale.* Turin: Einaudi, 2007.

Fadini, Ubaldo, ed. *Desiderio di vita: Conversazione sulle metamorfosi dell'uomo.* Milan: Mimesis, 1995.

Ferrajoli, Luigi. *Diritti fondamentali.* Rome: Laterza, 2001.

Fichte, Johann Gottlieb. *Sulla rivoluzione francese.* Rome: Laterza, 1966.

Forti, Simona. *Il tolitarismo.* Rome: Laterza, 2001.

Foucault, Michel. *The Birth of Biopolitics: Lectures at the Collège de France, 1978–1979.* Translated by Graham Burchell. New York: Palgrave Macmillan, 2008.

———. *The Hermeneutics of the Subject.* Translated by Graham Burchel. New York: Picador, 2005.

———. "Nietzsche, Genealogy, History." In *The Essential Foucault*, edited by Paul Rabinow and Nikolas Rose, 351–69. 1971. New York: The New Press, 2003.

———. *Security, Territory, Population: Lectures at the Collège de France, 1977–78.* Translated by Graham Burchell. New York: Palgrave Macmillan, 2007.

———. *Society Must Be Defended: Lectures at the Collège de France, 1975–76.* Translated by David Macey. New York: Picador, 2003.

———. "What Is Enlightenment?" In *The Foucault Reader*, edited by Paul Rabinow. New York: Pantheon Books, 1984.

Freud, Sigmund. *Totem and Taboo*. Vol. 14 of *The Standard Edition of the Complete Psychological Works of Sigmund Freud*. Edited by James Strachey. London: Hogarth Press, 1953–74.

Furet, Francois. *The Passing of an Illusion: The Idea of Communism in the Twentieth Century*. Translated by Deborah Furet. Chicago: University of Chicago Press, 1999.

Galli, Carlo. *Political Spaces and Global War*. Translated by Elisabeth Fay. Minneapolis: University of Minnesota Press, 2010.

Galzinga, Mario. *La malattia morale: Alle origini della psichiatria moderna*. Venice: Marisilio, 1988.

Gauchet, Marcel. "L'expérience totalitaire et la pensée de la politique." In *Retour du politique*. Paris: Esprit, 1976.

Gehlen, Arnold. *Man, His Nature and Place in the World*. Translated by Clare McMillan and Karl Pillemer. New York: Columbia University Press, 1988.

Girard, Rene. *Violence and the Sacred*. Translated by Patrick Gregory. Baltimore, Md.: Johns Hopkins University Press, 1984.

Goldmann, Lucien. *Introduction à la philosophie de Kant*. Paris: Gallimard, 1967.

Gunther, Hans Friedrich Karl. *Humanitas*. Munich: Lehmanns, 1937.

Heidegger, Martin. *Being and Time*. Translated by Joan Stambaugh. Albany: SUNY Press, 1996.

———. *The Fundamental Concepts of Metaphysics: World, Finitude, Solitude.* Translated by William McNeill and Nicholas Walker. Bloomington: Indiana University Press, 1995.

———. *Kant and the Problem of Metaphysics*. Bloomington: Indiana University Press, 1962.

———. "Letter on Humanism." In *Basic Writings*, edited by David Farrell Krell, 213–66. New York: Harper Collins, 1977.

Hitler, Adolf. *Libres propos sur la guerre et la paix recueillis sur l'ordre de Martin Bormann*. Paris: Flammarion, 1952.

———. *Mein Kampf*. 1943. Translated by Ralph Manheim. Boston: Houghton Mifflin, 1971.

Hobbes, Thomas. *Leviathan*. Translated by Edwin Curley. Indianapolis, Ind.: Hackett, 1994.

Holub, Robert. "Dialectic of the Biological Enlightenment: Nietzsche, Degeneration, and Eugenics." In *Practicing Progress. The Promise and Limitations of Enlightenment,*173–86. Amsterdam: Rodopi, 2007.

Kaminski, Andrzej. *I campi di concentramento dal 1896 a oggi.* Turin: Bollati Boringhieri, 1997.

Kant, Immanuel. "Bemerkungen zu den Beobachtungen über das Gefühl des Schönen und Erhabenen." In *Kant Gesammelte Schriften*, vol. 2, 205–56. Berlin: Akademie-Ausgabe, 1902.

———. "Conjectural Beginning of Human History." In *The Cambridge Edition of the Works of Immanuel Kant: Anthropology, History, and Education*, 163–75. Cambridge, UK: Cambridge University Press, 2009.

———. *Critique of Judgement.* Translated by James Creed Meredith. Oxford, UK: Oxford University Press, 2007.

———. *Critique of Practical Reason.* Translated by Werner S. Pluhar. Indianapolis, Ind.: Hackett Publishing, 2002.

———. "Critique of Practical Reason." In *Practical Philosophy*, edited by Mary J. Gregor. Cambridge, UK: Cambridge University Press, 1996.

———. "Idea for a Universal History with a Cosmopolitan Purpose." In *Political Writings*, edited by H. S. Reiss, 41–53. Cambridge, UK: Cambridge University Press, 1991.

———. "La religione nei limiti della semplice ragione." In *Scritti morali*, edited by P. Chiodi. Turin: UTET, 1970.

———. "Perpetual Peace: A Philosophical Sketch." In *Political Writings*, edited by H. S. Reiss, 93–130. Cambridge, UK: Cambridge University Press, 1991.

———. "Religion within the Boundaries of Mere Reason." In *Religion and Rational Theology*, edited by Allen Wood, 39–215. Cambridge, UK: Cambridge University Press, 1996.

———. "A Renewed Attempt to Answer the Question: 'Is the Human Race Continually Improving?'" In *Political Writings*, edited by H. S. Reiss, 177–90. Cambridge, UK: Cambridge University Press, 1991.

———. "What Does It Mean to Orient Oneself in Thinking?" In *Religion within the Boundaries of Mere Reason and Other Writings*, edited by Allen Wood and George Di Giovanni, 3–14. Cambridge, UK: Cambridge University Press, 1998.

Klee, Ernst. *Auschwitz, die NS-Medizin und ihre Opfer.* Frankfurt am Main: S. Fischer, 1997.

Klibansky, Raymond, Erwin Panofsky, and Fritz Saxl. *Saturn and Melancholy: Studies in the History of Natural Philosophy, Religion, and Art.* New York: Basic Books, 1964.

Lecourt, Dominique. *Humain, posthumain: La tecnique et la vie.* Paris: Presses Universitaires de France, 2003.

Lefort, Claude. *L'invention démocratique: Les limites de la domination totalitaire.* Paris: Fayard, 1981.

Lepenies, Wolf. *Melancholy and Society.* Cambridge, Mass.: Harvard University Press, 1992.

Lévinas, Emmanuel. "Some Thoughts on the Philosophy of Hitlerism." In *Unforeseen History,* translated by Nidra Poller, 13–21. Bloomington: University of Indiana Press, 2004.

Lifton, Robert Jay. *The Nazi Doctors: Medical Killing and the Psychology of Genocide.* New York: Basic Books, 1986.

Lisciani Petrini, Enrica. "Fuori della persona." *Filosofia politica* 3 (2007) 393–409.

Luhmann, Niklas. *Social Systems.* Translated by John Bednarz. Stanford, Calif.: Stanford University Press, 1995.

Lyotard, Jean-François. *The Differend: Phrases in Dispute.* Translated by Georges Van Den Abeelle. Minneapolis: University of Minnesota Press, 1988.

Mandelstam, Osip. *Tristia.* Barrytown, N.Y.; New York: Talman, 1987.

———. "The Twilight of Freedom." In *The Selected Poems of Osip Mandelstam,* translated by Clarence Brown and William Stanley, 22. New York: New York Review of Books, 2004.

Marammao, Giacomo. *Passaggio a Occidente: Filosofia e globalizzazione.* Turin: Bollati Boringhieri, 2003.

Marchesini, Roberto. *Post-human: Verso nuovi modelli di esistenza.* Turin: Bollati Boringhieri, 2002.

Maritain, Jacques. *The Rights of Man and Natural Law.* New York: Charles Scribner's Sons, 1943.

Marzocca, Ottavio. *Perché il governo.* Rome: Manifestolibri, 2007.

Masullo, Aldo. *La comunità come fondamento.* Naples: Libreria Scientifica Editrice, 1965.

Montani, Pietro. *Bioestetica.* Rome: Carocci, 2007.

Muller-Hill, Benno. *Murderous Science: Elimination by Scientific Selection of Jews, Gypsies, and Others; Germany 1933–1945.* Oxford, UK: Oxford University Press, 1988.

Nancy, Jean Luc. *The Experience of Freedom.* Stanford, Calif.: Stanford University Press, 1973.

———. *L'impératif catégorique.* Paris: Flammarion, 1983.

———. *The Sense of the World.* Translated by Jeffrey Librett. Minneapolis: University of Minnesota Press, 1997.

Nietzsche, Friedrich. *Frammenti postumi, 1881–82.* Vol. 5.2, *Opere.* Milan: Adelphi, 1964.

———. *Sämtliche Briefe.* Vol. 5.2. Munich and Berlin: de Gruyter, 1986.

Nolte, Ernst. *Der europäische Bürgerkrieg 1917–1945: Nationalsozialismus und Bolschewismus.* Berlin: Propyläen, 1987.

Nussbaum, Martha. *Sex and Social Justice.* Oxford, UK: Oxford University Press, 1999.

Onians, Richard Broxton. *The Origins of European Thought about the Mind, the Soul, the World, Time, and Fate.* Cambridge, UK: Cambridge University Press, 1988.

Pareyson, Luigi. *Ontologia della libertà.* Turin: Einaudi, 1995.

Philonekno, Alexis. *Théorie et praxis dans la pensée morale et politique de Kant et de Fichte en 1973.* Paris: Vrin, 1988.

Pico della Mirandola, Giovanni. *On the Dignity of Man.* Translated by Charles Glenn Wallis, Paul J. W. Miller, and Douglas Carmichael. Indianapolis, Ind.: Hackett 1998.

Plessner, Helmuth. *The Limits of Community: A Critique of Social Radicalism.* Translated by Andrew Wallace. New York: Humanity Books, 1999.

Proctor, Robert. *The Nazi War on Cancer.* Princeton, N.J.: Princeton University Press, 1999.

Ramm, Rudolf. *Arztliche Rechts- und Standeskunde: Der Arzt als Gesundheitserzieher.* Berlin: De Gruyter, 1943.

Reiter, Hans. "'La biologie dans la gestion de l'État.'" In *État et santé: L'image héréditaire de l'homme,* edited by Otmar von Verscheur, Leonardo Conti, and Hans Reiter, 12–31. Paris: Sorlot, 1942.

Rimbaud, Arthur. "Letter to Georges Izambard. Charleville, November 2, 1870." In *I Promise to Be Good: The Letters of Arthur Rimbaud,* translated by Wyatt Mason, 24. New York: Random House, 2004.

Rodotà, Stefano. *La vita e le regole: Tra diritto e non diritto.* Milan: Feltrinelli, 2006.

Rousseau, Jean-Jacques. *Émile: or, On Education.* Translated by Allan Bloom. New York: Basic Books, 1979.

———. *The Reveries of the Solitary Walker.* New York: New York University Press, 1979.

———. *Rousseau, Judge of Jean-Jacques: Dialogues.* Translated by Judith Bush, Christopher Kelly, and Roger Masters. Hanover, N. H.: University Press of New England, 1990.

———. *The Social Contract and the First and Second Discourses.* Edited by Susan Dunn. New Haven, Conn.: Yale University Press, 2002.

Sartre, Jean-Paul. *Existentialism Is a Humanism.* Translated by Carol Macomber. New Haven, Conn.: Yale University Press, 2007.

———. *No Exit, and Three Other Plays.* New York: Vintage, 1989.

Schiera, Pierangelo. *Specchi della politica: Disciplina, melancolia, socialità nell'Occidente moderno.* Bologna: Mulino, 1999.

Schmitt, Carl. *The Crisis of Parliamentary Democracy.* Translated by Ellen Kennedy. Cambridge, Mass.: MIT Press, 1988.

———. *The Nomos of the Earth in the International Law of the Jus Publicum Europaeum.* Translated by G. L. Ulmen. New York: Telos, 2003.

Singer, Peter. *Writings on an Ethical Life*. New York: HarperCollins, 2000.

Sloterdijk, Peter. *Die letzte Jugel: Zu einer philosophischen Geschichte der terrestrischen Globalisierung*. Frankfurt: Suhrkamp, 2002.

———. *Reglen für den Menschenpark*. Frankfurt am Main: Suhrkamp, 1999.

Starobinski, Jean. *History of the Treatment of Melancholy from the Earliest Times to 1900*. Basle, Switzerland: J. R. Geigy, 1962.

———. *Jean-Jacques Rousseau: Transparency and Obstruction*. Chicago: University of Chicago Press, 1988.

Talmon, Jacob Laib. *The Origins of Totalitarian Democracy*. Secker & Warburg: London, 1952.

Tauber, Alfred I. *The Immune Self: Theory or Metaphor?* Cambridge, UK: Cambridge University Press, 1994.

Thomas, Yan. "Le sujet du droit, la personne et la nature." *Le débat* 100 (1998): 85–107.

Tönnies, Ferdinand. *Community and Civil Society*. Translated by José Harris. Cambridge, UK: Cambridge University Press, 2001.

Vernes, Paul Monique. *La ville, la fête, la démocratie: Rousseau et les illusions de la communauté* Paris: Payot, 1978.

Vinale, Adriano, ed. *Biopolitica e democrazia*. Milan: Mimesis, 2007.

Weil, Simone. "Human Personality." Translated by Sian Miles. In *Simone Weil: An Anthology*, 49–78. New York: Grove Press, 1986.

———. "The Power of Words." In *Selected Essays 1934–1943*, 154–76. London: Oxford University Press, 1962.

Weindling, Paul. *Health, Race, and German Politics between National Unification and Nazism, 1870–1945*. Cambridge, UK: Cambridge University Press, 1989.